The Impressionists' Table

The Impressionists' Table

RECIPES & GASTRONOMY OF 19TH-CENTURY FRANCE

by Alexandra Leaf

❧

Wine Selections by Jacques Pépin

RIZZOLI
NEW YORK

For Chico Kasinoir
a true francophile and bon vivant

First published in the United States of America in 1994 by
Rizzoli International Publications, Inc.
300 Park Avenue South
New York, NY 10010

© 1994 Alexandra Leaf

94 95 96 97 98 99 / 10 9 8 7 6 5 4 3 2 1

Printed in Singapore

Design by Douglas & Voss, New York

Library of Congress Cataloging-in-Publication Data
Leaf, Alexandra
    The Impressionists' table: recipes & gastronomy of
19th-century France / by Alexandra Leaf; with wine
selections by Jacques Pépin.
        p. cm.
    Includes bibliographical references and index.
    ISBN 0-8478-1837-3
    1. Gastronomy—France—History—19th century. 2. Food
habits—France—History—19th century. 3. Cookery, French—
History—19th century. 4. Food in art. I. Title.
TX637.L39 1994
641'.01'30944—dc20   94–10790
                                                    CIP

Contents

ACKNOWLEDGMENTS

THERE ARE ALWAYS a great many people to thank when writing a book, and too little space in which to do it. I shall therefore resort to a group thanks to family members and friends who encouraged me, assisted me, inspired me, and in general helped me through the writing of this book.

Particular thanks go to my friends in Paris who extended great warmth and hospitality during my long stay there. I would like to give special thanks to S. G. Senders and Netty Maffert, the director and head librarian of the Bibliothèque Senders at the Institut Nationale Agronomique, where I did the bulk of my research. Their generosity, expertise, patience, and charm were greatly appreciated.

I am also indebted to the library staff at the New York Academy of Medicine for their always prompt and courteous assistance.

Thanks is owed to Daniel Boulud for his advice and interest in the book. A thank you is also owed to Beatrice Rehl who, from the very beginning, saw the possibilities for this book and gave me the courage to write it.

I would also like to thank my editor Manuela Soares for her valuable suggestions and comments and her unwavering faith in this project.

Gratitude is also owed to Jacques Pépin for his assistance with the wine selections and for his overall support and encouragement.

Thank you all.

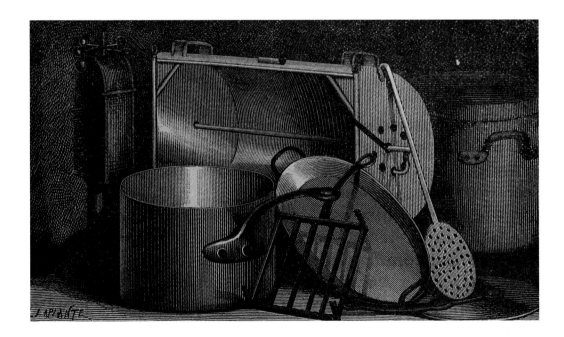

PREFACE

SOME TIME AGO, while taking a survey course on Impressionism, I became intrigued by the frequency with which the Impressionist painters depicted the French *à table*. Whether featuring Parisians quaffing beer in a brasserie, taking lunch at a restaurant along the Seine, or sipping absinthe at a café, these many scenes of dining seemed to reflect something new in France's food culture.

I felt that to really appreciate Pierre-Auguste Renoir's *Luncheon of the Boating Party* (1881) or Edouard Manet's *The Bar at the Folies-Bergère* (1881–82), more would have to be known about the dining practices of the French in the second half of the nineteenth century. This book, then, is my attempt to contextualize the popular and well-loved dining scenes of the French Impressionist painters.

The book is meant to evoke not only the French tradition of *le déjeuner sur l'herbe*—specifically the picnic scenes painted by Manet and Claude Monet—but also the gaiety and festivity so apparent in the numerous depictions of riverside boating-dining establishments along the Seine at Asnières, Bougival, and Chatou on the outskirts of Paris. In addition to picnics, café and restaurant scenes, and other images of dining, the book also contains an assemblage of vivid, richly textured still lifes of comestibles—fruits, vegetables, and fish—which have been underrepresented in discussions of Impressionism. In selecting the paintings contained here, I have, above all, sought to recapture the *joie de vivre* so evident in these portraits of the French table.

By documenting the steadily evolving state of gastronomy in France during the latter half of the nineteenth century, and exploring social change within French society at the time, we can account for the popularity of picnics, cafés, restaurants, and cafés-concerts as subject matter for such artists as Monet, Renoir, Manet, Vincent van Gogh, Henri de Toulouse-Lautrec, and to a lesser extent Edgar Degas, Mary Cassatt, and Berthe Morisot.

The book's coupling of the pictorial and culinary arts derives from the close and significant connection between dining, and specifically the café, and the Impressionist movement, for not only were the tenets of this new and controversial form of painting set forth and debated around café tables, but it was also in the cafés that many of the painters found models as well as clients, whose portraits they eagerly painted. Thus, by examining the works of the Impressionist painters that feature food themes, picnicking in the forest at Fontainebleau, or drinking beer at the Reichshoffen, much can be revealed about the changes in French dining practices at this fascinating time in history.

As for the recipes contained here, all are drawn from sources that date from the Impressionist epoch; the majority are culled from cookbooks in popular use at the time. Some, however, are the creations of the Impressionist painters themselves—namely, Claude Monet and Henri de Toulouse-Lautrec, who were avid cooks, first-class *amphitryons,* and gourmets of sorts.

And finally, by mining the literary output of such writers as Guy de Maupassant, Emile Zola, and others, and the writing of popular nineteenth-century literary gourmets, as well as immersing myself in gastronomical materials and accounts of French social life at the time of the Impressionists, I hope to shed light on a new aspect of a well-known, well-loved subject, the world of the Impressionist painters.

INTRODUCTION: À TABLE WITH THE IMPRESSIONISTS

IT IS WITH GOOD REASON that the nineteenth century was deemed the golden age of French gastronomy. It was the century *par excellence* of innovation in and expansion of many diverse aspects of the French table, from the growth of both the restaurant and cookbook industry, to the adoption of a new kind of table service for formal dinners. It was the century that produced such master chefs as Antonin Carême, Urbain Dubois, Jules Gouffé, and Georges Auguste Escoffier, and such literary gourmets as Jean-Anthelme Brillat-Savarin, Alexandre Dumas, and Alexandre-Balthazar-Laurent Grimod de la Reynière, whose unusual works extol the pleasures of the table. And as the vogue for dining out increased, whether eating *pâté en croûte* at Fontainebleau or taking lunch at a *guinguette* (open-air restaurant) along the Seine, the Impressionist painters responded to this increased food awareness by recording various scenes of dining.[1]

To more fully comprehend the nature of France's expanding food culture during the Impressionist era, it is necessary to consider certain changes within French society during the latter half of the nineteenth century. As bourgeois sociability shifted from the private realm of the family and community to the more public realm of parks, restaurants, brasseries, and boating establishments along the Seine, the café-restaurant became an extension of the home—a place where one could socialize, conduct business, hold informal gatherings, and of course dine.

Changes in France's demography and topography, particularly in Paris, had an impact on a newly evolving food industry. With Napoleon III's appointment in 1853 of Georges-Eugène Haussmann as prefect of Paris, the great French capital was to experience what came to be known as "the Haussmannization of Paris," the nineteenth century's version of urban renewal.[2]

Under Haussmann's direction, expensive apartment buildings and private mansions went up, replacing workers' housing and displacing inhabitants. Quais were built, and bridges were constructed over the Seine. Streets and avenues were widened, paving the way, quite literally, for the vast number of cafés, restaurants, cafés-concerts, and brasseries that would spring up to serve a city whose population had doubled between 1850 and 1880.

Under Haussmann, too, the legendary market known as Les Halles was constructed (1851–54). Operating as a wholesale market in the early hours and doing retail business later in the day, Les Halles provided Parisians with a myriad of foods from which to choose—exotic spices to Camembert cheese, *haricots verts* (string beans) to wild boar. In his 1873 novel entitled *Le ventre de Paris* (The Belly of Paris), Emile Zola set his story in the now-defunct food market. An immense still life—"*un poème gastrique*," as it was referred to by early critics—the novel is remarkable for its numerous descriptions of food.

Capturing the spirit of the great market as it must have been in the late 1800s, Zola describes its various pavilions for fruit, poultry and game, meat, fish, vegetables, and flowers, as well as the stalls that sold butter, eggs, cheese, and herbs. Zola delights in evoking the smell of overripe plums and conjuring up the purple-black hue of mussel shells and the blood-red color of a bushel of tomatoes.

Zola also succeeds in re-creating the harshness of the working conditions at Les Halles, helping us to understand the origins of the tradition of enjoying a

FACING PAGE: *Wine, swings, and games at Pinson's Guingette, Porte de Ménilmontant, c. 1880s. Musée Carnavalet, Paris*

Fish stall at Les Halles market, rue Rambuteau, 1898. Bibliothèque Nationale, Paris

steaming bowl of onion soup gratinée in the wee hours of the morning. As the workday at Les Halles began shortly after midnight, it was customary to warm oneself with a hot bowl of *soupe à l'oignon* served from great metal vats. And although the celebrated food market no longer exists, having been closed down in two phases between 1969 and 1973, the Parisian workers' custom of eating onion soup while the rest of the city lies sleeping has endured.

Another aspect of Haussmannization in Paris was the creation of broader streets and avenues. Of the city's newly widened boulevards, a Danish visitor wrote in 1889:

> The cafés form its main feature. They lie side by side, in countless number, along the thoroughfare between Bastille and the Place de la Concorde. . . . The café is a reserved seat in the street, a sort of comfortable sofa-corner in the great common parlor.[3]

For the young Impressionist painters, the cafés of Paris proved more interesting and instructive than the Ecole des Beaux-Arts or the exhibition halls (galleries as we know them today did not exist at the time). Serving as a kind of informal academy, the cafés provided a place for artists to gather to discuss their views on painting. It was at the Brasserie des Martyrs, one of the popular watering holes of the bohemian painters, where the Impressionists-to-be first encountered Gustave Courbet and Charles Baudelaire.

There, in the early 1860s, these young painters were to discover alternative approaches to the art mandated by the Académie des Beaux-Arts. At the Café Guerbois, as part of "Manet's circle," they were further exposed to Baudelaire's ideas about appropriate subject matter for "painters of modern life." Later, at the Café de la Nouvelle-Athènes, they would defend *plein air* (outdoor) painting.

LE CAFÉ GUERBOIS

AT THE GUERBOIS, about five o'clock in the afternoon, Edouard Manet frequently held court with a group of young painters who gathered around the café's marble-topped tables. Located on Avenue de Clichy, not far from Hennequin, Manet's paint supplier, the café attracted Edgar Degas, Pierre-Auguste Renoir, Frédéric Bazille, and Henri Fantin-Latour, and when they happened to be in Paris, Claude Monet, Paul Cézanne, Alfred Sisley, and Camille Pissarro. In attendance, too, were art critics and literary figures, most notably Emile Zola, an ardent defender of the Impressionists, and Félix Tournachon, known as Nadar, the journalist, cartoonist, and photographer.

Living and working in the Batignolles Quarter (near Montmartre in the northwest of Paris) as they did, these artists soon established regular Friday meetings at the café. So popular were their lively gatherings that two tables in the front room were set aside each week for *la bande à Manet*. Of these animated exchanges of opinion,

Monet recalled, "Nothing could be more interesting than these *causeries* with their perpetual clash of opinions. They keep our wits sharpened, they encouraged us with stores of enthusiasm that for weeks and weeks kept us up, until the final shaping of the idea was accomplished. From them, we emerged with a firmer will, with our thoughts clearer and more distinct."[4]

Several writers of the time paid homage to the Guerbois, featuring it in their stories. Zola, for example, describes the cafe in his 1886 novel *L'Oeuvre* (The Masterpiece), referring to it as the Café Baudequin; the novel's central character, an artist named Claude Lantier, is modeled after the writer's childhood friend, the painter Paul Cézanne. A devotee of the café, which Zola situated on the Boulevard des Batignolles, Lantier along with his painter friends would gather at the Baudequin at the end of a workday on Thursdays and also on Sundays. Although the café tables overflowed the canopied terrace onto the sidewalk, providing adequate seating in the clear, white sunlight outdoors, Lantier and his *bande* preferred the cool, deserted room at the back of the café, where they could "talk shop" undisturbed by the bustle of the boulevard.

The French writer Edmond Duranty, another member of the Impressionist circle of writers and critics, described the café in *La double vie de Louis Seguin* (The double life of Louis Seguin). Renaming it the Café Barbois, Duranty described the restaurant's altogether pleasant but curious atmosphere, detailing the sharp contrast between its front room, mirrored and glittering, resembling any number of fashionable boulevard cafés, and its low-ceilinged main room, adorned by six stocky columns, five billiard tables, waiters in long white aprons, and a great glass window that opened onto a garden.

LA NOUVELLE-ATHÈNES

BY 1876 THE CAFÉ GUERBOIS, with its pool players, had become too noisy, and the Impressionist painters abandoned

Café de la Nouvelle-Athènes, c. 1875. Bibliothèque Nationale, Paris

it in favor of the Nouvelle-Athènes on the Place Pigalle. There, the writers were in the majority: Duranty, Paul Alexis (a friend of Zola's), and the Irish novelist George Moore were regulars. Only Renoir, Manet, and Degas were habitués of the café; living outside of Paris, Monet, Sisley, Pissarro, and Cézanne made only rare appearances.

The Nouvelle-Athènes had a very pleasant terrace, which opened onto the Place Pigalle, making it an ideal spot for "people-watching." The Place Pigalle itself was heavily trafficked by a variety of artists, journalists, and writers, who lived in the area and who frequented the café in the evening. At the center of the Place Pigalle, in front of the fountain, a *foire aux modèles* was held each Monday, and artists came there in the hopes of finding the perfect likeness of Hercules, Venus, a vestal virgin, or a saint.

For the Impressionists, however, not only disinterested in mythological, religious, or historical subjects, but for the most part unable to pay a model the ten-franc fee for a sitting, it was usually necessary to recruit models from their friends and other habitués of the cafes. The model who posed for Manet's *The Bar at the Folies-Bergère* (1881–82), however, was chosen from those he saw at the Place Pigalle. Victorine Meurent, Manet's model for *Olympia* (1863), *Mlle. V. in the Costume of an Espada* (1862), and the universally known *Déjeuner sur l'herbe* (1863), was also recruited from the models at the Place Pigalle.

In writing of the significance of the Nouvelle-Athènes to the young Impressionist painters, George Moore recalled in his memoirs, *Confessions of a Young Man* (1888):

I did not go to either Oxford or Cambridge, but I went to the Nouvelle-Athènes. What is the Nouvelle-Athènes? He who would know anything

Le Café Tortoni, 1889. Bibliothèque Nationale, Paris

Edouard Manet, GEORGE MOORE AU CAFÉ, 1879. Oil on canvas. 25³/₄ × 32". Metropolitan Museum of Art, New York. Gift of Mrs. Ralph J. Hines, 1955

of my life must know something of the academy of fine arts. Not the official stupidity you read of in the daily papers, but the real French Academy, the café. The Nouvelle-Athènes is a café on the Place Pigalle . . . I can recall the smell of every hour. In the morning that of eggs frizzling in butter, the pungent cigarette, coffee and bad cognac; at five o'clock the fragrant odour of absinthe; and soon after the steaming soup ascends from the kitchen; and as the evening advances, the mingled smells of cigarettes, coffee, and weak beer. A partition, rising a few feet or more over the hats, separates the glass front from the main body of the café. The usual marble tables are there, and it is there we sat and aestheticized till two o'clock in the morning."[5]

Besides the Guerbois and the Nouvelle-Athènes, the cafés most closely linked to the history of Impressionism, a few other drinking and dining establishments in Paris are worth noting. The fashionable Tortoni, for example, on the Boulevard des Italiens, where *sorbet* was all the rage and proper attire *de rigeur*, attracted the dandy Manet, and he frequented this café-restaurant before establishing regular meetings at the Guerbois. Of

Tortoni's popularity, a nineteenth-century observer wrote,

> ... this establishment was so much in vogue that it was difficult to get an ice there; after the opera and theatres were over, the boulevards were literally choked up with the carriages of the great people of the court and the Faubourg St.-Germain bringing their guests to Tortoni's.[6]

There was also the Brasserie Reichshoffen on the Boulevard Rochechouart, which is believed to be the setting for Manet's *Corner of a Café* (1879); it was one of the barmaids at the Reichshoffen who served as the model for the painting. Beer consumption was on the rise in Paris, and Manet was to exploit the vogue for this formerly "working-class" beverage in three works: *Le Bon Bock—The Engraver Bellot at the Café Guerbois* (1873), *At the Café* (1878), and *Women Drinking Beer* (1878).

Au Père Lathuille

In the Batignolles Quarter, not far from the Guerbois or the Nouvelle-Athènes, was the Père Lathuille, a *guinguette* and restaurant whose popularity dated from the beginning of the century. Manet chose the restaurant's garden terrace as the setting for *Chez le Père Lathuille* (1879), a painting he hoped would be approved that year by the Salon's jury.

The work contains two central figures, a young man crouching at a table occupied by an older woman. The proprietor's son, Louis Gautier-Lathuille; Ellen Andrée, an actress; and Judith French, a cousin of the composer Jacques Offenbach, all served as models for the painting. The canvas, which was in fact accepted for the official Salon of 1880, aptly conveys the atmosphere of a respectable dining establishment, where one might have found *Potage aux Légumes* (vegetable soup), *Fonds d'Artichaut Farcis* (stuffed artichoke hearts), *Poulet Sautée Père Lathuille* (a sautéed chicken specialty), and *Poires Bourdaloue* (pears with frangipane cream) on the menu.

Cafés, brasseries, and restaurants proliferated in post–Haussmannian Paris (the city could name some 30,000 true cafés by 1895, up from 4,000 in 1869). In addition, cabarets and cafés-concerts, or *caf'-conc's* as they were nicknamed, became popular as places where one could dine lightly and be entertained. The evolution of cafés and brasseries to caf'-conc's, where song and dance entertainment was provided, began in the 1840s and continued throughout the next two decades.

Theatrical events were presented on either small indoor stages or in open-air gardens or pavilions. Both indoor and outdoor caf'-conc's charged extra for the entertainment by either raising the prices of their drinks or by charging an admittance fee. Among the most popular of these entertainment halls were the Ambassadeurs and the Alcazar d'été, both of which were depicted by the Impressionist painters, in particular by Renoir and Degas.

The caf'-conc's were soon to compete with the music halls, which quickly grew in popularity at this time. Not too unlike the caf'-conc's, but with dancing of a much more exuberant kind, the music halls eventually offered short operettas, farces, commercial ballets, and various kinds of circus and vaudeville acts.

This was the era, too, of the French can-can and the *chahut*—two frenetic dances that had all of Paris mesmerized. Mark Twain recalled an evening spent at the Jardin Mabille, one of the most popular dancing spots of the time:

> The dance had begun . . . I backed up against the wall of the temple, and waited. Twenty sets formed, the music struck up, and then—I placed my hands before my face for very shame. But I looked through my fingers. They were dancing the renowned 'Can-can' . . . The idea of it is to dance as wildly, as noisily, as furiously as you can; expose yourself as much as possible if you are a woman; and kick as high as you can, no matter which sex you belong to. There is no word of exaggeration in this.[7]

and hot chocolate, the Moulin de la Galette was situated on a plot of land upon which stood two windmills (*moulins*). No longer in operation, the site had been converted into an open-air dance hall, where popular balls were held each weekend.

In an attempt to safeguard the reputation of the establishment, unaccompanied women and women without hats were not permitted; eventually both men and women were required to wear hats—even while they danced. Unlike men, who were charged an admittance fee of twenty-five centimes, women were admitted free of charge so long as they were accompanied by a gentleman. (Toward the close of the century, this had changed and men were charged fifty centimes to enter and women half that amount.) In his marvelous portrait of Parisian leisure, *Dance at the Moulin de la Galette*, Renoir features carefree couples dancing in the sun-dappled garden and other young men and women seated at tables before their partially consumed drinks. The atmosphere is happy and relaxed, suggesting nothing of the frenzy of the Jardin Mabile.

Having determined to paint his picture out of doors at the site of the ball itself, Renoir rented a studio nearby at 12 rue Cortot and transported the canvas to the Moulin de la Galette each day assisted by two friends. And there, during the fall of 1875, he created his masterpiece, aided by the young neighborhood women and their boyfriends, who served as eager models.

AUX FOLIES-BERGÈRE

EQUALLY AS WELL KNOWN and well loved as Renoir's painting of the Montmartre dancing spot is Manet's *The Bar at the Folies-Bergère*. Located at the time near the rue Bergère in the ninth *arrondissement* (district) in Paris, the music hall takes its name from the eighteenth-century *folie*, an open-air spot for dancing, drinking, and entertainment. Opening in the rear of a department store in 1863 as a *salle de spectacles*, the entertainment hall became so successful that in 1871 it was bought by the colorful

Entrance to the gardens of the Moulin de la Galette, c. 1880s. Bibliothèque Nationale, Paris

LE MOULIN DE LA GALETTE

ANOTHER POPULAR DANCING SPOT, possibly the best known for its depiction by Renoir, was the Moulin de la Galette. Located in the newly annexed Montmartre section of Paris, this open-air dancing establishment was the setting for one of Renoir's most spectacular paintings, *Dance at the Moulin de la Galette* (1876). Named for the *galettes* (round flat cakes made of puff pastry) that were served with drinks, usually beer, wine, liqueurs, coffee,

Ladies of the town at the Moulin Rouge, Montmartre, c. 1900. © Collection Roger-Viollet

entrepreneur Léon Sari, who remodeled it and created two large spaces out of the one.

There was a great hall with balconies known as the Jardin (garden), which was covered only by an awning. The other space was a U-shaped theater with a balcony overhead. Recognizing that the sale of alcohol would yield great profits, Sari installed bars on both floors and set up tables and chairs on the ground floor. As a means of increasing alcohol sales, Sari hired attractive young women, many of whom were aspiring actresses, to work as *verseuses,* or barmaids. In Paris during the latter half of the nineteenth century, women were increasingly hired to work in cafés and brasseries as this female presence proved beneficial to alcohol sales.[8]

Unlike Renoir's painting of a working-class dance hall, Manet's features an establishment that was, for the most part, reserved for the well-to-do. Here one could sip Veuve Cliquot or Mumm champagne, rum, port, cognac, and beer, as well as sweeter, lighter *liqueurs de dames* such as Grand Marnier, Cointreau, and cassis, and any number of Grand Cru wines. One could also lightly dine on oysters, caviar, smoked salmon, and consommé, and be entertained by operettas, troupes of comedians, and acrobats who swung from trapezes overhead. An admission fee of two francs was charged for the cheapest seats and five francs for reserved seats.

Le Moulin Rouge

THERE WAS ALSO LE MOULIN ROUGE, which during the latter half of the nineteenth century was renowned not only for its superb entertainment but also for the fare served at its restaurant. Habitués of the establishment at its original site at the Rond Point on the Champs Elysées included Emile Zola, Gustave Doré, Alphonse Daudet, the Goncourt brothers, and Henri de Toulouse-Lautrec, who was perhaps its best-known customer. In 1883, however, the Moulin Rouge closed its doors as a restaurant *cum* theater, and reopened in 1889 as a dance hall catering to all classes of entertainment seekers.

A popular French newspaper wrote about the hall's reopening on October 6:

> Last night the whole of Paris was there to celebrate the opening, and the show was not only on the stage, but also in the audience. On view were Their Highnesses Prince Stanislas de Pontiatowski and Prince Troubetzkoi, the Compte de la Rochefoucauld, Messieurs Elie de Talleyrand, and Alexandre Duval, the creator of the famous clear soups, together with the flower of literature and the arts, having the time of their lives. Picture carriage parties arriving from the chic districts of Neuilly and Passy, hobnobbing happily with natives from lower Montmartre and

George Auriol (Jean-Georges Huyot).
MENU FOR LE CHAT NOIR, *before 1895.* Worcester Art Museum, Worcester, Massachusetts, Eliza S. Paine Fund

Rochechouart, clothcapped roughs and young women with unkempt hair, knotted in a bun . . .[9]

The lively and festive atmosphere of the Moulin Rouge greatly attracted Toulouse-Lautrec, who painted and sketched numerous works of the legendary dance hall. Whether featuring can-can dancers, female clowns, or top-hatted gentlemen with elegantly attired companions, Lautrec captured the ambiance of this great theater. Although when it reopened it no longer served food, the Moulin Rouge still served a full range of drinks from *eau de Seltz* (seltzer water) to Veuve Cliquot, *vin ordinaire* (table wine) to fine brandies and liquors.

Judging from the menu at Le Chat Noir, a popular Montmartre cabaret, the fare at these cafés, bars, cabarets, and music halls was usually limited to light foods such as oysters, caviar, crayfish, onion soup or consommé, cold roast chicken, grilled or roasted meats, ham, sausage or Gruyère cheese sandwiches, and omelettes, both savory and sweet, such as ham, cheese, *aux fines herbes* (assorted herbs), *au sucre* (sugar), or *au rhum* (rum). And as many cafés-concerts and music halls had first-rate wine cellars, there was always an ample selection of drinks.

Guinguettes on the Seine

By the close of the century, Paris was overflowing with any number of establishments where one could sample a variety of wines, beer, cider, absinthe, *digestifs*, and robust cuisine. Quite popular, too, were the *guinguettes* on the outskirts of Paris, for there, beyond the city limits, liquor was not taxable. On Sundays, such establishments, which had sprung up in Asnières, Bougival, Chatou, and other Seine-side spots, teemed with Parisians who had fled the city for a bit of fresh air and romance.

A mere ten-minute train ride from the Gare Saint-Lazare in Paris, Asnières was the first stop on the Seine northwest of the city. A village whose population had increased from 1,300 in 1856 to 15,200 thirty years later, Asnières was the answer to the Parisians' growing appetite for leisure. From early on, the town's principal attractions were its boating, its Sunday festivals, and its *bals* (dances). There, one could row, sail, swim, shoot, picnic, dance, stroll, and dine at the château of Asnières, which had been converted into a restaurant. There were regattas to attend, concerts, cafés-concerts, circuses, fairs, and produce markets. One could also sample the fare—fried fish Seine-style, sandwiches of ham and Gruyère cheese, *gaufres* (dessert waffles), and fruit tarts—from the many vendors of hot and cold food who catered to the multitudes of pleasure seekers.

Because of its proximity to Paris, Asnières rather quickly became overdeveloped and overfrequented, causing many Parisians as well as the Impressionists themselves to seek out other Seine-side spots. Bougival, Chatou, and Croissy Island to the west of Paris, though easily accessible due to expanding train lines from the Gare Saint-Lazare, were still far enough away from the city to have preserved great green swards amid the loading docks, chalk quarries, and sawmills that flanked the banks of the river.

La Grenouillère

During the summer of 1869, Monet and Renoir were drawn to Croissy Island, and more specifically to the rowdy and colorful resort La Grenouillère. This most Parisian of bathing places was immortalized by the two painters in their twin depictions, both entitled *La Grenouillère*. Nicknamed the "frog pond" because of the many "available" young women (*grenouilles*) who went there, Croissy was a twenty-minute train ride from the Gare Saint-Lazare to either Reuil or Chatou, and then a walk or carriage ride of a mile or so.

The restaurant at this popular riverside establishment was fashioned out of two old barges, which were moored beneath shade trees. On top of the barges, a simple shelter had been constructed for open-air dining and dancing. Access to the *café flottant* was across a footbridge, which was connected to a small, round island known as the "Camembert" because of its resemblance in configuration to the French cheese. The island was also nicknamed the "Pot à Fleurs," because of the tree that grew from its center. This tiny island was connected by a narrow footbridge to Croissy Island.

La Grenouillère was the creation of an enterprising carpenter known as Père Seurin, who foresaw the potential of a riverside establishment in close proximity to Paris. Capitalizing on the fact that many pleasure seekers came to spend a day, week, or month on the island, Seurin set up tables and seats, boathouses, changing

37. CHATOU — Restaurant Fournaise et la Seine

Le Restaurant Fournaise on Croissy Island on the River Seine at Chatou. Association des Amis de La Maison Fournaise

rooms, and cabins along the banks of the Seine; food and drink were sold beneath the trees, and boats and bathing costumes were rented to these vacationers. Swimming lessons in the clean, open waters of the river at Chatou were also available.

Seurin held a weekly dance on Fridays and provided a five-piece orchestra, which played to the energetic crowds. In the evening, Parisians, locals, and boating enthusiasts from up and down the Seine gathered at this voguish floating *guinguette* and danced quadrilles and waltzes in the open air. The establishment was enclosed only by a tarpaulin roof and illuminated in the evening by colored Chinese lanterns, whose light was reflected in the water below. In one of his short stories entitled "La femme de Paul," Guy de Maupassant described the guinguette's setup, and the stark contrast between the wildly exuberant atmosphere of the dance floor at night and the tranquillity of the star-strewn sky just outside.

LE RESTAURANT FOURNAISE

NEARBY, ALSO ON CROISSY ISLAND, was another popular dining and rowing establishment, Le Restaurant Fournaise.[10] Best known for its depiction in *Luncheon of the Boating Party* (1881) by Renoir, the restaurant's atmosphere was not entirely different from that of La Grenouillère. Alphonse Fournaise's restaurant catered for the most part to the *canotiers* (canoeists); some came there by boat from other riverside spots in the environs of Paris, while others came seeking to rent one of the many canoes offered by Fournaise.

Fournaise's river-side restaurant became quite popular among the Parisian upper classes, and it was not uncommon to see finely dressed men and women, nobility included, amid the bare-armed, undershirt-clad canoeists dining on *Soupe au Chou* (cabbage soup), *Omelette au Lard* (bacon omelet), *Friture de Seine* (fried fish Seine style), *Poulet ou Gigot Roti* (roast chicken or leg of lamb), and *Salade de Pommes de Terre* (potato salad)—washed down no doubt by a good Bordeaux.

Those who came to dine *chez* Fournaise were served on the canopied terrace of his riverside restaurant. For the 100-sous menu he offered his guests, Alphonse Fournaise also provided at midday, a majestic view of sunlight flickering on the Seine, and a veritable parade of 300 to 400 boats passing beneath the newly reconstructed bridge at Chatou. And there, *en plein air* beneath the terrace's red and white striped awning, Renoir painted his famous portrait of Seine-side dining.

Maupassant à Table

ONE OF FOURNAISE'S MOST DEVOTED FANS, an avid rower and *sportif*, was Guy de Maupassant. His short stories, although written several years after the heyday of Impressionism, are vignettes of Parisian leisure at the time of the Impressionists. His volume of collected works entitled *La maison tellier* features several stories that readily capture the ambiance of an outing to the countryside *au bord de la Seine*. The stories, which describe afternoons of dining and rowing on the Seine, can in many ways be seen as literary counterparts to Renoir's *Luncheon of the Boating Party* (1881), *Oarsmen at Chatou* (1879), and *The Canoeists' Luncheon* (1879–80).

Set at La Grenouillère, Le Restaurant Fournaise, and on Croissy Island, the sometime haunts of Monet and Renoir, these stories contain lively descriptions of the fare served at these and other popular Seine-side dining spots. In "Une Partie de Campagne," Maupassant describes the Dufour family's Sunday lunch at a Seine-side dining spot on the outskirts of Paris, not far from Asnières. Opting to forego table and chair and have a picnic on the grass, the family orders "*une friture de Seine, un lapin sauté, une salade et du dessert*" (fried fish Seine style, sautéed rabbit, salad, and dessert), accompanied by several bottles of Bordeaux.

In another story entitled "Yvette," Maupassant describes the kinds of drinks that were served at the floating café at La Grenouillère. Seated at tables at this "*ponton à consommations*" (refreshment pontoon), those who have come to drink and forget quaff "white, red, yellow, and green liquids." In describing beverages of these colors, it can be assumed that Maupassant was referring to white wine or *pastisse* (an anise-flavored aperitif), red wine, beer, and absinthe, all of which could have been served *chez* Seurin.[11]

By setting his colorful stories at La Grenouillère, so often featured by Monet and Renoir, Maupassant establishes a link between food and art in the late nineteenth century.

Painting and Dining: Celebratory Meals

THE PICTORIAL AND CULINARY ARTS in France are further linked during the Impressionist period by the annual tradition of dining out after attending the Salon on opening day. In the Palais de l'Industrie, where the yearly art exhibition was held each May, a restaurant had been constructed where fashionable ladies and gentlemen could choose from such dishes as *Poulet Chasseur* (chicken hunter's style), *Filets Mignons Sauce Béarnaise* (filet mignon with béarnaise sauce), *Boeuf Braisé* (braised beef), and *Oeufs aux Pointes d'Asperges* (eggs with asparagus tips). In another part of the Salon restaurant, one could opt for lighter, more economical fare such as a sandwich of Gruyère cheese, roast beef, or ham, a brioche, a cup of coffee, or a glass of wine.[12]

One could also lunch in any number of eateries in the vicinity of the Palais de l'Industrie. The nearby Le Doyen on the Champs Elysées was another popular après-Salon spot; each May, on the day that the Salon opened, Edmond de Goncourt would dine there with Zola and other Parisian literati. The main attraction at Le Doyen was its lovely garden in spring, with fountain and flowering chestnut trees. The restaurant's house specialty, *Sole Soufflé Le Doyen*, also proved to be quite a draw. According to chronicles of the time, one could actually eat better and more reasonably at other boulevard restaurants—but the setting *chez* Le Doyen was far lovelier.

During the late years of Impressionism, when the painters were no longer plagued by financial problems, they went to some of Paris's better restaurants, including Le Doyen. Claude Monet, for example, with an art critic friend, Gustave Geffroy, instituted their "Friday Diner Drouant," gathering at a restaurant called Drouant with Auguste Rodin, Edmond de Goncourt, Toulouse-Lautrec, and his friend the art dealer Maurice Joyant. There, they dined on *Bécasse, façon de la Maison Drouant* (woodcock Drouant style), *Grives à la Polonaise* (thrushes sautéed in champagne with truffles and cured ham), and *Poires Josette* (a frozen confection of poached pears, vanilla ice cream, and *crème Chantilly*). Renoir and Gustave Caillebotte preferred to dine at the Café Riche, where they would meet on the first Thursday of each month. Such restaurants as Magny, Julien, Prunier, Le Café Anglais, and Le Café de Paris were also frequented by the more well-to-do painters.

CHEZ MONET AT GIVERNY

THE MOST SERIOUS GOURMETS among the Impressionist artists themselves were Monet and Toulouse-Lautrec. At his enchanted home in Giverny, just far enough from Paris to offer the painter the seclusion he sought, Monet saw to it that the table was a central part of his and his family's existence. Along with his second wife, Alice Hoschedé, Monet, or most often his cook Marguerite, would prepare a variety of dishes whose ingredients came straight from their vegetable gardens, fruit trees, and farmyard.

The principal meal of the day was lunch, served at 11:30 A.M. sharp. Artists and writers such as Renoir, Sisley, Pissarro, Whistler, Rodin, Maupassant, and Paul Valéry, as well as art dealers and collectors who had come from Paris to visit the painter's studio, were often invited to join Monet for lunch. The meal was usually composed of a hot first course, perhaps stuffed tomatoes or mushrooms *au gratin*, followed by a meat or fish dish, a cooked vegetable, a salad, and dessert.

The evening meal started with soup—a mixed vegetable or a leek and potato soup, for example—followed by an egg or cheese dish. Then came the main course, which was sometimes poultry, a *Poulet Chasseur* or a chicken braised in red wine, or a dish of cold meat, plus a salad and cheese—Roquefort, Camembert, Gruyère, or Brie. Dessert usually consisted of whatever cake or sweetened bread had been prepared for the noon meal, or a compote of peaches, cherries, or plums made by Marguerite.

Monet's great love of food dates from his trips in 1858 to Honfleur in Normandy with his painter friends Eugène Boudin and Johann Barthold Jongkind. At La Ferme Saint-Siméon, an inn of sorts run by a farmer named Toutain and her daughter, Monet painted the surrounding countryside and feasted on a variety of fish and seafood dishes that could not have been fresher, such as *Poulardes à la Crème* (chicken in a rich cream sauce) and homemade *cidre*.[13]

The cooking journals kept by Monet include recipes from friends, recipes from restaurants in Paris that he frequented, and recipes collected during his travels abroad. They reflect the artist's deep love for carefully prepared food.[14]

Dîner des Tarnais

One of Toulouse-Lautrec's humorous illustrations for a menu commemorating a dinner for his countrymen from the Tarn region of southern France. Musée Toulouse-Lautrec, Albi

Toulouse-Lautrec and the Art of Cuisine

Toulouse-Lautrec considered cooking an art like any other, and a dish, an artistic creation comparable to a poem or ballet. Cooking was, above all, an art of living, meant to be shared with family and friends. Having been raised in a household where culinary matters were given utmost attention, Lautrec developed a flair for cooking and entertaining at an early age. Together with Maurice Joyant, the art dealer and Lautrec's lifelong friend, Lautrec held countless dinners to which music hall dancers, art collectors, artists, and Parisian intellectuals were all invited.

The painter often shocked visitors to his studio, for besides being a workplace, it was also a bar, so well stocked that he could offer guests almost any cocktail. He maintained that to properly contemplate a painting, it was necessary to have a drink in hand. Lautrec also stated that only wine was the proper accompaniment to a meal; water, he claimed, ruined the palate. So adamant was he in his belief that Lautrec often placed carafes of water containing live goldfish on the table.

Lautrec also believed that the most successful meals were those which were well organized and where great importance was attached to the appearance of both table and menu. When entertaining, Lautrec and Joyant preferred to hold luncheons rather than dinners, as they felt guests could appreciate a meal at midday better than one in the evening, when they would be tired after a day of work.

A luncheon, Lautrec maintained, should consist of only two main dishes, one rather more elegant than the other so that it stood out as the centerpiece of the meal. These two dishes were accompanied by side dishes, which worked together to form a balanced, "harmonious" meal.

For Lautrec, every artistic expression was cause for a culinary celebration, itself announced by a festively decorated menu or illustration. The artist always offered his guests a menu listing the dishes to be served that day printed on a watercolor, a drawing, a sketch, or a lithograph.

When vacationing with Joyant, Lautrec fished and hunted and then produced original culinary creations, which he enjoyed with whomever was about. Of his travels with Lautrec, Joyant recalled, "Around him, dishes and ideas proliferated: whether it was in Brussels, London, or in his habitual quarters of Paris and Arcachon, succulent and simple dinners were improvised in honor of the guests, the chosen of both sexes."[15]

On one of their vacations together, as the only passengers on a cargo ship traveling between Le Havre and the port city of Dakar in Senegal, Lautrec and Joyant insisted that they be taken ashore along the Brittany coast "to inspect the fishing boats and to take on a cargo of lobsters and quivering fish." "The boiler room," wrote Lautrec, "was transformed into a kitchen. We opened cases of old port and fine olive oil . . . which, with premeditation, accompanied the baggage of these modern pirates [the ship's crew one assumes] who gorged themselves on vast quantities of lobsters à l'américaine."[16]

There are many anecdotes about Lautrec's adventures in the kitchen. He was once engaged by his friend Alexander Natanson to cater a party in celebration of the artist Edouard Vuillard. The invitation to this soirée, designed by Lautrec, was sent to 300 guests requesting their company at half past eight in the evening for "American and other drinks." His head shaved, wearing a waistcoat fashioned out of the stars and stripes of an American flag, Lautrec served as barman, dispensing drinks all evening to the painters, writers, publishers, and actors in attendance.

Accompanying the vast array of cocktails, some in shot glasses, others layered in brilliant colors (Lautrec designed the drinks for their visual impact as well as their intoxicating effect), were a variety of salty foods and spicy dishes. Lautrec claimed that although he poured over 2,000 drinks that evening, reducing his guests to a drunken stupor, he remained sober all the while.

Whether catering a party or cooking at home on Avenue Frochot in Paris, Lautrec's love and knowledge of the culinary arts were evident. And as a true *gourmand* and gourmet, Lautrec always carried a little grater and whole nutmeg to flavor the glasses of port he so enjoyed.

RENOIR THE PURIST

WHILE RENOIR COULD INDEED APPRECIATE *la bonne chair* (good food), as is evidenced by his monthly dinners with Caillebotte at the Café Riche, his approach to food was somewhat different from that of either Monet or Lautrec. Unlike these two painters, who were deeply interested in the culinary arts and liked to experiment in the kitchen, Renoir was, in his attitude toward food and its preparation, a purist—just as he was in other aspects of his life. He believed that food was at its best when cooked in casseroles or earthenware pots, and vegetables were to be cooked *à la vapeur*, steamed on a wood-burning stove. (Gas stoves, which were already popular by the third quarter of the nineteenth century, were unacceptable to him.) For the painter, the proper way to cook meats was to roast them on a spit, and butter was to be bought fresh in a mound from a *crémerie*, not in a packaged slab or bar. Bread, Renoir claimed, should never be cut in slices but should be broken in pieces, and fruit was to be peeled only with a silver-bladed knife. *Oh, les beaux jours!*

COOKBOOKS IN NINETEENTH-CENTURY FRANCE

THE ATTENTION PAID TO FOOD by Monet, Toulouse-Lautrec, and Renoir—the interest in quality, the instinct to record recipes, and the desire to expand one's culinary repertoire—was hardly limited to a select few. An interest in the skillful preparation of food, as well as the art of dining on the part of these artists, may be seen as a reflection of a general increased awareness of culinary matters that took hold in France during the latter half of the last century. And a significant result of this new consciousness was the proliferation of cookbooks and monthly food publications for both the home cook and the professional.

Georges Vicaire's *Bibliographie gastronomique*, "a bibliography of books appertaining to food and drink and related subjects from the beginning of printing to 1890," reveals the extent of this development. From roughly midcentury onward, there is a veritable boom in the publication of *almanachs, manuels, guides,* and *traités* on food.

Among the most widely used of these guides were Gaston Martin's *Le livre de tous les ménages* (published successively from 1857–67), Cauderlier's *L'économie culinaire* (1861, 1864, 1889), Mme. C. Durandeau's *Guide de la bonne cuisine* (1887), *Le livre de cuisine* by Jules Gouffé, "l'ancien

JULES GOUFFÉ
ANCIEN OFFICIER DE BOUCHE DU JOCKEY-CLUB DE PARIS

LE LIVRE DE CUISINE

LA CUISINE DE MÉNAGE ET LA GRANDE CUISINE

LIBRAIRIE HACHETTE ET Cⁱᵉ
1913, Paris, Bᵈ St-Germain, 79

Title page of the 1913 edition of Gouffé's LE LIVRE DE CUISINE

These guides and manuals provided a great deal more than just directions for the preparation of a variety of dishes. In many instances, the recipes were preceded by extensive notes on the seating of guests for formal dinners (including the suggestion that diners be placed at a distance of two feet [60 cm] from one another), the responsibilities of the host or hostess to their guests, and the importance of punctuality on the part of the guests, as causing a dish to wait would greatly insult the chef. Directions were given on how to clean and polish silver and glassware. Diagrams and illustrations were included to instruct the home cook on how to properly carve and serve a variety of meats, poultry, and fish. Information on what kinds of kitchen utensils were necessary to equip a kitchen and how to use them was often included, as well as explanations on the use of different kinds of pots, pans, baking dishes, and molds.

Nutritional information was frequently provided, and menus were often presented to help both *ménagère* (housewife) and *gastronome* (gourmet) plan balanced meals. In the case of Baron Brisse's formidable cookbook, a menu was featured for each day of the year including leap year, thus the figure of 366. The majority of cookbooks produced during this period stressed the importance of economizing, to the extent that thrift was elevated to the status of virtue. As a result, a number of cookbooks were published on "*l'art d'accommoder les restes,*" the art of using leftovers. Suzanne Alfred's *Cent manières d'utiliser les restes* (1892) was among the most popular of these books.

As literacy increased among women in France in the nineteenth century, so did sales of cookbooks. And indeed women became the primary readership. Part of the appeal of cookery books of the time was their function as demystifiers, as they could explain how dishes were prepared—dishes that were consumed by the well-to-do at home and in Paris's finest restaurants. With a bit of skill and luck, the *ménagère* might be able to re-create something of the splendor of those dishes heretofore in reach of only the wealthiest individuals.

officier de bouche du Jockey Club de Paris"¹⁷ (first published in 1867), Urbain Dubois's *La cuisine classique* (first published in 1854; 12th edition, 1886), and his *Nouvelle cuisine bourgeoise pour la ville et pour la campagne* (8th edition, 1888), Léon Brisse's *Les 366 menus de Baron Brisse avec 1,200 recettes et un calendrier nutritif* (12th edition, 1881), and Louis Eustache Audot's *La cuisinière de la campagne et de la ville* (which went into its 79th edition in 1901).

For all the information it attempted to convey, however, the nineteenth-century French cookbook was often very vague with respect to quantity of ingredients and manner of preparation. Whereas today's recipes are quite specific, nineteenth-century recipes frequently called merely for "some carrots," "the right amount of salt," "a good piece of butter," or "a glass of oil." The lack of specificity of these early recipes appears to result from the assumption that the nineteenth-century cook, already quite competent in the kitchen, needed only general directions for the preparation of a dish.

It is interesting to note that among the earliest advocates of greater precision in recipes was Jules Gouffé, a pastry chef. At a time when recipes were still very general, directions for pastry making were already rather precise with respect to measurement and manner of preparation—a result of the greater need for precision in baking. Gouffé's cookbooks are striking in the precise, almost scientific approach to measurements he employs.

Although written more than a century ago, Gouffé's recipes appear almost modern when compared with those of his contemporaries. In the introduction to *Le livre de cuisine: La cuisine de ménage et la grande cuisine* (1867), he lamented the proliferation of cookbooks claimed by their authors to be "new and improved." In his eyes these were simply a recycling of old recipes, imprecise with respect to quantity and cooking time, and therefore unsuitable as guides for the home cook as well as the professional.

The nineteenth-century recipe also differs from that of today's recipe in terms of form; the modern recipe allows the cook to determine, at a glance, what ingredients are called for because ingredients are set forth separately from the directions. The nineteenth-century recipe, however, was organized as a single, continuous paragraph, often surprisingly brief, where ingredients and directions were listed together. It is therefore striking to compare Gouffé's recipes with those of his contemporaries, for the specifications of

LES 366 MENUS

1ᵉʳ JANVIER.

Potage à la Condé.
Barbue à la béchamel.
Aloyau au vin de Madère.
Poulets rôtis à la peau de goret.
Artichauts à la barigoule.
Baba au rhum.

Potage à la Condé. — C'est une purée de haricots rouges bien cuits, détendue avec du bouillon et passée au tamis de soie. Versez-la dans une soupière sur des croûtons de pain frits au beurre et servez.

Barbue à la béchamel. — Faites-la dégorger deux heures à l'eau fraîche ; égouttez-la et couvrez-la de sel blanc. — Une heure après, plongez-la dans de l'eau salée en ébullition, et laissez-la cuire durant 20 à 25 minutes, mais à petit feu de peur qu'elle ne se fende, servez avec une sauce à la béchamel.

Poulet rôti à la peau de goret. — Faites rôtir en broche un poulet. Vers la fin de sa cuisson, placez à l'extrémité d'un hâtelet un morceau de lard enveloppé de papier, mettez le feu au papier qui, en brûlant, fondra le lard et laissez dégoutter sur le poulet. Ces gouttes brûlantes déterminent à la peau du poulet des boursouflures semblables à celles qui se produisent sur la peau du cochon de lait pendant qu'il rôtit.

Artichauts à la barigoule. — Parez et ratissez blanchir à l'eau les artichauts et remplissez-les d'une farce composée de champignons , échalotes et persil hachés et lard râpé, le tout assaisonné et passé au beurre. Pour les cuire, les ficeler, les mettre dans une casserole entourés de bardes de lard, les arroser d'huile et les laisser mijoter ; servir sur leur sauce réduite.

This menu for the first of January from LES 366 MENUS DE BARON BRISSE *(1875) features hearty winter fare. From the first course to dessert, the dishes include a soup of puréed red beans, brill (a European flat fish) with a bechamel sauce, sirloin steak in a Madeira wine sauce, spit-roasted chicken, artichokes with bacon and herbs (see recipe on page 86), and rum cake (see recipe on page 64).*

quantity and the vertical format he employs make his recipes look rather more contemporary than nineteenth century.

LÉGUMES   357

les pois dans une passoire, et trempez-les simplement à l'eau chaude. — Chauffez dans une casserole 2 cuillerées de sauce blonde et un morceau de
beurre; ajoutez les pois, sel et une pincée de
sucre; chauffez-les 2 minutes, en les sautant;
liez-les alors avec 2 jaunes d'œuf étendus avec
un peu de bouillon, mêlés avec 60 grammes de
beurre divisé en petites parties.

PETITS-POIS A LA FRANÇAISE.

Mettez les pois dans une casserole avec un
morceau de beurre, un peu d'eau froide, un bouquet composé d'oignons verts et persil, un peu de
sel, une pincée de sucre. Couvrez et cuisez 7 à 8
minutes à feu vif; retirez-les sur feu plus doux.
Quand ils sont cuits, retirez-les du feu et liez-les
simplement avec du bon beurre, un peu abondant; servez les sans faire bouillir.

PETITS-POIS ET POMMES DE TERRE AU BEURRE.

Faites bouillir de l'eau dans une marmite en
terre; ajoutez un litre de gros pois frais et ten-
dres, une vingtaine de pommes de terre nouvelles
avec la peau, mais lavées, un peu de sel, un oignon et un bouquet de persil : pommes de terre
et pois doivent se trouver cuits en même temps.
Egouttez-les. Pelez les pommes de terre; mettez-
les dans un plat avec les pois; arrosez-les avec du
bon beurre fondu et abondant; servez.

CHOUX-FLEURS A LA SAUCE.

Prenez un chou-fleur, retirez-en les feuilles vertes, et divisez-le par bouquets; lavez-les; échau-
dez-les à l'eau bouillante, puis, plongez-les dans
casserole d'eau chaude. Cuisez-les à couvert jus-
29.

LÉGUMES.   251

Lorsque les artichauts sont ainsi préparés, ayez de la friture
que vous essayerez avec la mie de pain, comme il est dit à l'ar-
ticle *Friture* (page 108), et qui ne fasse que grésiller très-dou-
cement.

Il ne faut pas que la friture soit trop chaude; on y met
l'artichaut cru, et il ne doit pas prendre couleur avant d'être
cuit.

Lorsque les artichauts sont frits, égouttez-les, salez-les et
dressez-les en rocher;

Garnissez de persil frit, et servez.

PETITS POIS A LA FRANÇAISE.

Soit 1 litre de pois fins et toujours fraîchement écossés.

Mettez-les dans une casserole, d'une contenance de 2 litres;
lavez et égouttez.

Ajoutez :

    100 grammes de beurre,
      1 décilitre d'eau,
     50 grammes d'oignons blancs,
      1 pincée de sel,
     25 grammes de sucre.

Quelques personnes ajoutent du persil, nous le proscri-
vons absolument. Il ne sert, suivant nous, qu'à dénaturer le
goût des pois, qu'on ne saurait trop conserver dans toute la
pureté.

Mettez-les à feu modéré pendant 30 minutes, la casserole
bien couverte;

Quand ils sont cuits, ajoutez-y 100 grammes de beurre ma-
niés avec 20 grammes de farine, puis retirez-les du feu;

Agitez la casserole en tournant pour bien mêler; s'ils sont
trop liés, mettez un quart de décilitre d'eau froide;

Goûtez; s'ils ne sont pas suffisamment sucrés, ajoutez 5 grammes de sucre.

Lorsqu'on emploie les pois de conserve, on les lave à l'eau
bouillante, on les égoutte, on les assaisonne comme les pois
frais.

Under the heading LEGUMES *(vegetables) in his*
NOUVELLE CUISINE BOURGEOISE
POUR LA VILLE ET POUR LA CAMPAGNE *(1888),*
Urbain Dubois presents several recipes for
brussels sprouts, green peas, and cauliflower.
Note Dubois's single paragraph, short format compared with
Gouffé's more contemporary, explicit style.

In this recipe for Petits Pois à la Française from
Jules Gouffé's LE LIVRE DE CUISINE *(1870),*
the chef's precision is in evidence.
Although he wrote the recipe over a hundred years ago,
it has a strikingly modern look compared with
other recipes of the time.

LITERARY GOURMETS: GRIMOD DE LA REYNIÈRE, BRILLAT-SAVARIN, & ALEXANDRE DUMAS

IN ADDITION TO THE HOW-TO COOKBOOKS of Gouffé, Brisse, Dubois, and Durandeau, other kinds of food writing was being done in the nineteenth century. The increased food awareness that the Impressionist artists reflected in their paintings, led gourmand and gourmet alike to pen essays and poems in praise of the French table. Among the earliest of these literary gourmets was Alexandre-Balthazar-Laurent Grimod de la Reynière (1758–1838), who was affectionately dubbed *"le père de la table"* ("the father of the table") by nineteenth-century French critic Charles Augustin Saint-Beuve. His *Almanach des gourmands,* which was published annually from 1804 to 1812, was a slim, pocket-size volume containing essays on particular foods, humorous cartoons of boisterous individuals eating to their hearts' content, and accounts of banquets held for and by Parisian glitteratti.[18]

Another early chronicler of *la littérature gastronomique* and a contemporary of Grimod was Jean-Anthelme Brillat-Savarin (1755–1826), author of *La physiologie du goût: Méditations de gastronomie transcendante.* The book won him immediate praise when it was first published in 1825. (The work is still being published today.) Dedicated by its author to Parisian gastronomes, this highly unusual work contains Brillat-Savarin's musings on countless aspects of gastronomy, from how to make a tuna omelette to the mechanism of taste.

As Brillat-Savarin's approach was in many instances that of a scientist, the book includes, in addition to strictly culinary matters, his ideas about the effects of fasting on the body, and the causes and nature of obesity and anorexia. Besides these scientific proclamations, practical information is given on the preparation of a variety of foods including game. In addition, the addresses of Paris's finest specialty food stores, Madame Chevet's *magasin de comestibles* at the Palais Royal and the pastry shop "Achard," are provided.[19]

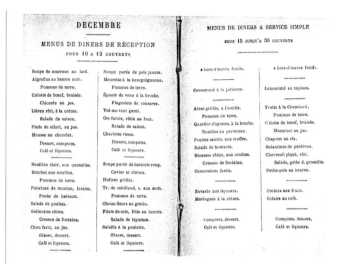

In these menus for December, Urbain Dubois features two types of dinners, one designed for roughly a dozen guests and the other for larger numbers. Note how many dishes comprise just one menu.

Alexandre Dumas (1802–70), author of *The Three Musketeers* and *The Count of Monte Cristo,* also figures importantly among these nineteenth-century food writers for his monumental book *Grand dictionnaire de cuisine.* As the author's last work before his death in 1870, this encyclopedia-like document of some 600,000 words serves to a certain extent as a gauge by which to measure the scope of French cuisine at midcentury. Beginning with "absinthe," the poet's "Green Muse," and ending with an entry defining "zest," this weighty book provides useful general information on the raising of animals for slaughter and on the preparation of a vast array of comestibles, from almonds, anchovies, and anise to whiting, wild chicory, and woodcock.

Although not well received when it was published in Paris in 1873, possibly because it was considered to be long-winded and of little practical value, Dumas's 1,198-page "national gastronomic monument," deservedly takes its place beside the writings of Brillat-Savarin and

Grimod de la Reynière. Whatever its shortcomings, the book serves in part to illustrate the scope of foods available to the French at the time of the Impressionists.[20]

A CHANGING FOOD CULTURE:
SERVICE À LA FRANCAISE OR SERVICE À LA RUSSE

LIKE THE WRITINGS of Grimod de la Reynière, Brillat-Savarin, and Dumas, and the cookbooks of Gouffé, Dubois, and Martin, the Impressionist painters' depictions of *flâneurs* and *demi-mondaines* strolling along café-lined boulevards, or picnic parties in woodsy spots near Paris point to France's expanding food culture in the nineteenth century. Their works reflect principally the outward changes within this emergent food culture—the popularity of dining out and the dramatic increase in the number of cafés and restaurants. At the same time, though, the paintings of Monet, Manet, Renoir, Mary Cassatt, Berthe Morisot, and others reflect in subtler ways shifts that were taking place in French society, the reverberations of which could be felt in the kitchen.

An important area of change at this time was the table service for formal dinners served at home. The dominant type, known as *service à la française*, was slowly being replaced by *service à la russe*. It should be noted here that formal dinners in nineteenth-century France included a number of services, each consisting of several courses. Each course, in turn, was composed of various dishes from among which guests would choose.

With *service à la française*, all of the dishes in a particular *service* were placed on the table at one time regardless of whether they were meant to be eaten hot or cold, and guests would choose from among them; often, the dishes comprising the first service were already on the table when the guests were seated.

Service à la russe, unlike French service, involved serving dishes one after another, presenting them individually to each diner, thus showing off the talent of the chef. This method was also more practical as it allowed large cuts of meat to be carved and garnished in the kitchen, away from the gazes of guests. Moreover, food that was intended to be eaten warm could be, as hot dishes were brought out at the moment they were to be served. Russian service enabled food to be eaten under the best conditions, as it was cooked, carved, served, and eaten without delay.

A formal French dinner at midcentury might have consisted of the following: a first service (*Potages*) composed of a choice of several kinds of soup; simple or elaborate hot and/or cold items (*hors d'oeuvres*) such as pâté, stuffed olives, and marinated oysters, a variety of dishes (*relevées de potages*) that might include vegetables, rice, or noodles; and another assortment of dishes (*entrées*) usually hot, quite like the preceding course. The second service (*Rôtis*) was made up of several roast game and meat dishes—partridge, quail, hare, duck and pheasant, veal, ham, pork, and lamb—which were generally accompanied by salads. Sometimes fish dishes were also served during this course.

The third service (*Entremets*) was comprised of a wide variety of fish, vegetable, and egg dishes such as *Truite Frite* (fried trout), *Choux de Bruxelles à la Maître d'Hôtel* (brussels sprouts with butter and herbs), *Tomates Farciés à la Provençale* (stuffed tomatoes Provençal style), or *Oeufs Brouillés aux Pointes d'Asperges* (scrambled eggs with asparagus tips). This service also included *entremets sucrés*, which were sweet dishes such as plum pudding, dessert omelettes, rice pudding, crêpes, and a number of different kinds of cakes.

The fourth service (*Dessert*) consisted of an assortment of fresh fruits and/or fruit compotes, cakes and pastries such as baba au rhum, madeleines, chocolate cake, almond cake, waffles, and macaroons. Whipped cream and fruit jellies (*gelées et confitures*) made from cherries, raspberries, apricots, grapes, plums, and quinces were also included in this service. And cheeses, such as Roquefort, Camembert, Brie, and Gruyère, might also be offered as part of the dessert.

It was customary to drink Madeira, Marsala, or vermouth after the soup course. With the *relevées* and with both hot and cold entrées in the first service, such Burgundies and Bordeaux wines as Beaune, Saint-Emilion, Pommard, Mouton-Cadet, and Château Lascombe were served. Before the second service was brought out, Château Yquem and Rhine wines were served slightly chilled to freshen up the diner's palate. With the *Rôtis* of the second service through the *entremets de légumes*, other Burgundies and Bordeaux, such as Chambertin, Clos Vougeot, Château-Lafite, Château-Margaux, and Haut-Brion, were poured. The preferred manner of serving wines, from midcentury onward, involved the guests serving themselves, passing the bottles from hand to hand; this was the accepted practice for champagne as well.

To accompany the *entremets de douceur*, the sweet dishes eaten during the third service, sherry was served. And with the fourth service, such dessert wines as Tokay, red and white muscats, and Alicante, made from Grenache grapes, were offered. When the meal was over, guests were ushered into the living room where coffee was served along with liqueurs—cognac, Cointreau, Grand Marnier, liqueur de cassis, and port wines. About an hour later, *eau sucré*, water sweetened with sugar, was brought out and served in small glasses.

In the planning of menus, whether for a formal dinner or a simple luncheon containing only one service and dessert, certain dietary restrictions regarding fast days (*maigre*) and nonfast days (*gras*) were applied. *Gras* referred to dishes that contained meat and *maigre* to dishes without it, which were thus permissible for Catholics on Fridays or other fast days. Many cookbooks of the time indicated beside each recipe whether it was *gras* or *maigre*, and often proposed alternate versions of a sauce, one containing meat and the other not. In *Le livre de cuisine*, Jules Gouffé presents a recipe for *Potage aux Epinards* (spinach soup) and suggests that if the soup is to be made *maigre*, cream added at the very end (moments before serving so that it does not cook) may be substituted for the beef or chicken bouillon.

As may well be imagined, the custom of dining *à la française* was enjoyed only by the very wealthy who, regarding it as symbolic of their elevated status, were reluctant to adopt the simpler, less dazzling Russian service. Among the Impressionist painters, it seems likely that only those with privileged backgrounds, Manet, Degas, Morisot, and Caillebotte and only much later Monet and Renoir, would have enjoyed the kinds of meals that have been described here. The shift away from a formal manner of dining, with *service à la russe* replacing *service à la française*, can be seen as part of a general relaxation of strictures within French society during the latter half of the nineteenth century—a relaxation of social norms that the Impressionist artists recorded in their paintings.

The pleasures of Parisian tables were much celebrated during the Impressionist era. Whether depicting the *canotiers* sipping wine and reposing along the banks of the Seine, or featuring Parisians taking lunch at an outdoor café, these portraits of dining are a reflection of the change occurring in France's food culture at the time.

As cafés and restaurants grew in number and popularity among the French, dining as subject matter for the Impressionist painters also increased in popularity. In their attempts to record various aspects of the everyday life of the "modern" individual, Manet, Monet, Renoir, Toulouse-Lautrec, Degas, Cassatt, and Morisot have left behind a gastronomical legacy that, along with the output of cookbook writers and literary gourmets of the day, illuminates a significant aspect of the Impressionist epoch—the French *à table*.

NOTES

1. See Barbara K. Wheaton, "The Pleasures of Parisian Tables," in *The Pleasures of Paris: From Daumier to Picasso* (Boston: Museum of Fine Arts, Boston, and David R. Godine, 1991).

2. For a discussion of the Haussmannization of Paris, see T. J. Clark's brilliant study of nineteenth-century Paris and its environs, *The Painting of Modern Life: Paris in the Art of Manet and His Followers* (Princeton: Princeton University Press, 1984).

3. Quoted in *The Pleasures of Paris: From Daumier to Picasso*, p. 49.

4. John Rewald, *The History of Impressionism* (New York: Museum of Modern Art, 1973, 4th edition), p. 197.

5. George Moore, *Reminiscences of the Impressionist Painters* (Dublin, 1906).

6. *Reminiscences and Reflections of Captain Gronow*, 1862, quoted in *The Pleasures of Paris: From Daumier to Picasso.*

7. Mark Twain, *The Innocents Abroad* (New York: NAL-Dutton, 1966).

8. See Clayton Hollis, *Painted Love* (New Haven and London: Yale University Press, 1991), for a discussion of the role and status of women working in these *brasseries à femmes.*

9. Jacques Pessis and Jacques Crepineau, *The Moulin Rouge* (Gloucestershire: Alan Sutton, Ltd., 1990), p. 12.

10. Fournaise's establishment was recently restored and reopened as Le Restaurant Fournaise. Its open, airy setting along the banks of the Seine makes it a lovely dining experience as part of an afternoon's outing from Paris. Address: Ile des Impressionistes, 78400 Chatou, France. Telephone: 011-33-1-30-71-41-91.

11. For further reading on absinthe consumption in France in the nineteenth century, see Barnaby Conrad's marvelous social history of the drink, *Absinthe: History in a Bottle* (San Francisco: Chronicle Books, 1988).

12. See Wheaton, "The Pleasures of Parisian Tables."

13. La Ferme Saint-Siméon has been restored and converted into a magnificent hotel-restaurant. It is open year-round and well worth a visit. Address: Rue Adolphe-Marais, 14600 Honfleur, France. Telephone: 011-33-31-89-23-61.

14. The cooking journals of Claude Monet have been published in English as *Monet's Table* by Claire Joyes (New York: Simon and Schuster, 1989). This lovely book, a translation of *Les carnets de cuisine de Monet* (1989), not only contains a variety of Monet's favorite recipes, but also presents a portrait of the artist's life amid his family, friends, and gardens at Giverny.

15. Maurice Joyant and Henri de Toulouse-Lautrec, *The Art of Cuisine* (New York: Henry Holt, 1966), n.p.

16. Ibid.

17. The term "officier de bouche," literally translated as "officer of the mouth," came into use in France around the sixteenth century. The title was conferred upon an individual possessing outstanding culinary sensibilities, as an "officier de bouche" was responsible for everything that pertained to the table . . . and the mouth. From selecting the dishware to choosing the wines, and from overseeing the kitchen and pantry to approving the menu, this was the domain of the "officier." Today the title is no longer used, having been replaced by the term "maître d'hôtel," which has been shortened to simply "maître d'." On the title page of his cookbook, *Le livre de cuisine,* Jules Gouffé boasts to his readers that he is the former maître d' of the Jockey Club, one of Paris's better addresses in Gouffé's time.

18. On all subjects pertaining to food, Grimod de la Reynière wrote vividly and affectionately. Baron Brisse features the literary gourmet's "*éloge des pâtés de*

légumes" (eulogy of vegetable pâtés) in his menu for the 18th of August:

> *Pendant les rigueurs du carême et les jours maigres, ce mets est une excellente ressource pour les maîtresses de maison. Les petits pois, les jeunes fèves de marais, les carottes naissantes, les haricots verts dans toute leur tendreté, soit frais, soit conservés, peuvent se dessiner en compartiments dans une belle croûte de patisserie, et présentent un mets d'autant plus savoureux que la crème qui fait la base de leur assaisonnement flatte agréablement le palais.*

During the rigors of Lent and lean days, this dish is an excellent resource for mistresses of the house. The green peas, the young broad beans from the marshes, the baby carrots, the string beans in all their tenderness, either fresh or preserved, may be laid out in compartments in a lovely pastry shell, and make for a dish all the more flavorful because the cream that forms the basis of its seasoning delights the palate most agreeably.

19. Brillat-Savarin is also well remembered for his marvelous, often witty aphorisms. Of the truffle and its treasured status he once wrote: "There are two breeds of truffle eaters, one which believes that truffles are good because they are expensive, and the other that knows they are expensive because they are good." And on the subject of the responsibilities of a host to his guest, Brillat-Savarin wrote: "*Convier quelqu'un, c'est se charger de son bonheur pendant tout le temps qu'il est sous votre toit.*" (To extend an invitation to someone is to take responsibility for his happiness all the time he is under your roof.)

20. For a discussion and critique of *Grand dictionnaire de cuisine,* see Alan Davidson's essay "Alexandre Dumas and *Le Grand dictionnaire de cuisine*" in the *Journal of Gastronomy* (Summer 1990). Also of interest is *Dumas on Food: Recipes and Anecdotes from the Classic Grand Dictionnaire de Cuisine,* translated by Alan and Jane Davidson (New York and Oxford: Oxford University Press, 1978).

AUTHOR'S NOTE: It is necessary, as part of a discussion of gastronomy in France at the time of the Impressionists, to make some mention of the harsh effects of the seige of Paris on the capital's food supply during the Franco-Prussian War (1870–71). Edmond de Goncourt's journals provide a vivid and heart-rending portrait of the extreme privation suffered by Parisians during the five-month siege. In early entries Goncourt notes which foods were no longer obtainable and how these changes were reflected in the restaurants' bills of fare. Strikes were waged against butchers as people demanded that cattle be sold directly to them instead of going through those "speculators in human misery" who made hefty profits on the meat they managed to procure.

Horse meat slipped into the Parisian diet, and within a month, it was being sold throughout Les Halles. Instead of butter, beef or horse fat in large, yellowish squares was proffered. Vegetables such as cabbage, celery, and cauliflower were still in good supply. On October 29, Goncourt wrote: "Je mange ce soir du filet d'âne (donkey)." Cats, dogs, and rats were soon served up. Cats went for six francs apiece and rats for one franc each. Dog cutlets, which according to Goncourt were really quite appetizing for their resemblance to mutton chops, went for one franc a pound.

As Parisians desperately sought out other sources of animal protein, the tragic, yet inevitable took place. Buffalo, antelope, kangaroo, and elephant, former residents of the Paris Zoo, appeared on the menus of fashionable Parisian restaurants. On December 31, Goncourt wrote: "At Voisin's this evening I see the famous elephant blood sausage again; indeed I dine on it."

The most readable account in English of the siege is Otto Friedrich's *Olympia: Paris in the Age of Manet* (New York: Harper Collins, 1992). Readers of French should go directly to Goncourt's journals. Also in French, excerpted for ready access, are the relevant entries from Goncourt's journals found in Robert Courtine and Jean Desmur's *Anthologie de la littérature gastronomique: Les Écrivains à table* (Paris: Editions de Trevise, 1970).

16 Mars 1895
53, Rue Rodier

MENU

La Bouillabaisse

Hors d'œuvre

Salmis de Perdrix bojé tzaria Krani

L'Agnelet roti

Le Sarigue en Liberty

Salads

Foies gras de l'oïe Fuller

Vegetables

Pièce humide

Cheese and Fruits

Ti Noir

Pivre Lilas Frotteurs

&

Champagne Charlie

A NOTE ABOUT THE RECIPES

IN COMPILING THE RECIPES contained here, I have concerned myself mainly with authenticity; each featured recipe was in use in France at the time of the Impressionist painters. The sources of these recipes are varied and range from the personal cooking journals of Claude Monet and Henri de Toulouse-Lautrec to popular French cookbooks of the time.

To facilitate the preparation of the dishes presented in this book, all recipes have been adapted to meet the needs of the contemporary cook and kitchen. To have given the recipes in their original nineteenth-century, vague yet nonetheless charming, state would have rendered them less accessible to the modern-day cook. Reprints of recipes by Jules Gouffé, Urbain Dubois, and Baron Brisse, however, give the reader a feel for what a nineteenth-century recipe was like.

The amplitude of the menus featured here reflects a style of eating that belongs more to the past than to the present. Each menu, consisting of seven to eight dishes, involves a greater amount of food than the average person would consume in today's health and diet-conscious age. Predating "nouvelle" trends in cooking as they do, many recipes featured appear quite rich. Each cook, however, may opt for lighter versions of these recipes by substituting vegetable or olive oil where appropriate and omitting cream sauces, thereby reducing the overall fat content.

In creating the menus for each section, it has been my intention to recapture the spirit of a meal at the time of the Impressionists. The dishes chosen were either specialties of the epoch, specialties of the painters themselves, or signature dishes of popular restaurants of the time. If a complete menu seems too rich or too complex to prepare at one time, the cook may pick and choose from among the dishes. One may select a soup, a vegetable dish, one entrée, and a dessert and then in essence have two menus of four dishes for each one I have created.

In selecting the dishes to create a harmony and balance of flavors for each menu, the cookbooks of Urbain Dubois, Jules Gouffé, and Baron Brisse proved especially helpful. Not only were they useful in gaining a sense of the scope and range of the nineteenth-century menu in France, they were, above all, highly inspirational.

Jacques Pépin's expertise in French food and wine, coupled with his deep knowledge of the culinary history of France in the nineteenth century, were of invaluable assistance. He has listed the wines in the order in which they should be drunk; that is, the first wine accompanies the appetizer and/or the main course, and the second, the dishes that follow.

This book is a portrait of an era that existed more than a hundred years ago—a time that differs largely from our own, but still has certain parallels in the culinary domain. Just as food, whether newly cultivated or newly imported, along with cafés and restaurants, occupied an increasingly important place in the lives of nineteenth-century men and women, so it does for us today. The publication of vast numbers of cookbooks in the nineteenth century also very much parallels our situation today.

Like our counterparts depicted in the works of the Impressionist painters, we are passionate about food and delight in its preparation, whether at home or dining out. Though our world bears little resemblance to that of Manet, Monet, Renoir, or Morisot, we are nonetheless able to recognize something of ourselves in their joyful paintings of riverside dining, picnicking in a forest, or cherry picking on a summer's day. Bon appétit!

[MENU № 1]

Luncheon of the Boating Party

Moules Marinière Comme aux Halles
MUSSELS MARINIÈRE LES HALLES STYLE

Aubergines Frites
FRIED EGGPLANT

Filets de Sole au Vin Blanc
FILLET OF SOLE IN WHITE WINE

Gigot Rôti
ROAST LEG OF LAMB

Salade d'Endives
ENDIVE SALAD

Fromages Assortis
ASSORTED CHEESES: BRIE, GRUYÈRE, GOAT CHEESE

Tarte aux Abricots et aux Pêches
APRICOT-PEACH TART

Vins
WINES
Muscadet de Sèvre-et-Maine / Cornas (Côtes du Rhône)

Café et Liqueurs
COFFEE AND LIQUEURS

THIS MENU PAYS HOMAGE to Impressionism's quintessential dining establishment—Le Restaurant Fournaise—located in Chatou on the outskirts of Paris. The hotel-restaurant served simple, hearty fare prepared by Alphonse Fournaise's wife and served by his daughter, Alphonsine. The menu features some of the restaurant's specialties: *Gigot Rôti*, *Tarte aux Fruits*, and other popular dishes of the time.

MOULES MARINIÈRE COMME AUX HALLES / MUSSELS MARINIÈRE LES HALLES STYLE
ADAPTED FROM URBAIN DUBOIS'S *La cuisine classique*, 1886.

This recipe honors Emile Zola, whose evocative descriptions of mussels, shellfish, and other foodstuffs fill the pages of his novel *Le ventre de Paris.* Mussels were widely enjoyed in France during the nineteenth century, and this preparation was among the most popular. Another common method of serving mussels was in a fish broth thickened with cream and egg yolks (*potage aux moules*).

Serves 4–6

4	TABLESPOONS UNSALTED BUTTER
¼	CUP CHOPPED ONION
1	CUP MINCED SHALLOTS
4	QUARTS MUSSELS, CLEANED
1 ½	CUPS DRY WHITE WINE
1	SPRIG FRESH THYME
1	SMALL BAY LEAF
2	TABLESPOONS CHOPPED FRESH PARSLEY
½	TEASPOON SALT
	FRESHLY GROUND BLACK PEPPER

In a large pot, melt 2 tablespoons of the butter and add the onion and shallots. Cook for a few minutes, then add the mussels, wine, thyme, bay leaf, parsley, salt, and pepper. Cook, covered, over high heat for 5–10 minutes, or just long enough for the shells to open. Prepare a broth by straining the pan liquid through cheesecloth to catch whatever sand may remain at the bottom. Add the remaining butter to the strained liquid. Transfer the mussels to a serving dish. Discard any with unopened shells. Pour the broth over the mussels and serve.

AUBERGINES FRITES / FRIED EGGPLANT
ADAPTED FROM MÉLANIE CARÊME'S *Le parfait Cordon Bleu*, c. 1870.

Serves 4

2	MEDIUM-SIZE EGGPLANTS
	SALT
	VEGETABLE OIL FOR FRYING
	JUICE OF ½ LEMON
	PARSLEY SPRIGS (GARNISH)

Peel the eggplants and cut into thin slices. To drain off excess moisture before cooking, sprinkle the eggplant slices with salt and let stand for about 20 minutes. Drain the eggplant and pat dry with paper towels. In a large skillet, heat the oil to 375°F, add the eggplant slices, and fry until golden on both sides. (If you don't have a frying thermometer, test the oil by adding a slice of eggplant. If it turns golden quickly, the oil is hot enough.) Remove with a slotted spoon and drain on a dish lined with paper towels.

When the eggplant has drained, transfer to a serving dish lined with a napkin or paper towel. Season with salt and lemon juice. Place several sprigs of parsley around the eggplant slices and serve very hot.

37. CHATOU — Restaurant Fournaise et la Seine

FILETS DE SOLE AU VIN BLANC / FILLET OF SOLE IN WHITE WINE

ADAPTED FROM JULES GOUFFÉ'S *Le livre de cuisine*, 1867.

Fish was an indispensable component of a formal meal in the nineteenth century. Lighter and easier to digest than other animal proteins, fish dishes were believed to offer diners a "break" after game was served and to enliven their appetites before eating meat dishes. In *Le livre de Cuisine*, under the heading SOLE, Gouffé provides twenty-seven recipes for this fish; Dubois features twenty-four in *La cuisine classique*.

Serves 4

    4   LARGE SOLE FILLETS
    3   TABLESPOONS UNSALTED BUTTER
    2   TABLESPOONS MINCED SHALLOTS
         SALT
         FRESHLY GROUND BLACK PEPPER
    ½   CUP DRY WHITE WINE
    ¼   CUP CRÈME FRAÎCHE (RECIPE FOLLOWS)
    1   TEASPOON MINCED CHIVES (GARNISH)

Preheat the oven to 350°F.

Grease a large baking dish and place the fillets inside. Dot with 2 tablespoons of the butter and sprinkle with the shallots. Season with salt and pepper, and slowly pour the wine over the fish. Cover with aluminum foil and bake for about 20 minutes. When the fish is cooked, transfer the cooking juices to a saucepan. Reduce this liquid over high heat to about ⅓ cup. Stir in the *crème fraîche* and bring the mixture to a boil, beating with a wire whisk. Remove from the heat and add the remaining tablespoon of butter to the sauce. Transfer the fish to a heated serving dish and cover with the sauce. Sprinkle chives on top of the fish and serve at once.

CRÈME FRAÎCHE

In many supermarkets, in addition to specialty food stores, *crème fraîche* is now available. If you cannot find it, make your own. Not only is it very simple to prepare, it keeps well in the refrigerator for at least a week. Here are two preparations that are equally tasty and simple to make.

Crème Fraîche I

Makes 2 cups

    1   CUP SOUR CREAM
    1   CUP HEAVY CREAM
         (PREFERABLY NOT ULTRA-PASTEURIZED)

In a bowl, mix the 2 creams together until well blended. Place the bowl in a plastic bag so that it is loosely covered. Set the bowl in a warm place that is free of drafts. Let stand overnight. When the mixture has thickened, refrigerate for several hours before using. The cream will develop a tarter flavor as it sits in the refrigerator.

Crème Fraîche II

Makes 1 cup

    1   CUP HEAVY CREAM
         (NOT ULTRA-PASTEURIZED)
    1   TABLESPOON BUTTERMILK

In a small bowl, mix the cream and buttermilk together. Cover the bowl well with plastic wrap and set in a warm place overnight. When the cream has thickened, it can be used right away or refrigerated for future use.

GIGOT RÔTI / ROAST LEG OF LAMB
ADAPTED FROM GOUFFÉ'S *Le livre de cuisine*, 1867.

Revealing his love of language, Dumas had the following to say about lamb in his *Grand dictionnaire de cuisine*: "The name of this charming little animal [*agneau*] is said to have a most poetic origin. According to the bucolic etymologists, it comes from the verb *agnoscere*, to recognize, because when it is tiny it recognizes its mother. In fact, when it can barely walk it follows its mother, tottering and bleating."

Serves 6–8

1	LEG OF LAMB (4–5 POUNDS)
¼	CUP VEGETABLE OR OLIVE OIL
3	CLOVES GARLIC, MINCED
2	SPRIGS FRESH ROSEMARY
	SALT
	FRESHLY GROUND BLACK PEPPER
	ROSEMARY SPRIGS (GARNISH)

In a bowl, combine the oil, garlic, rosemary leaves, salt, and pepper. Rub the mixture all over the lamb and marinate for several hours or overnight.

Place the lamb in a shallow roasting pan and let the meat stand at room temperature for 1 hour. Preheat the oven to 450°F. Place the lamb in the center of the oven and roast for 10 minutes. Reduce the temperature to 350°F and cook another hour or so, depending on the desired degree of doneness. When meat is cooked, let it stand for 20 minutes before carving. Garnish with fresh rosemary sprigs.

SALADE D'ENDIVES / ENDIVE SALAD
ADAPTED FROM CAUDERLIER'S *L'économie culinaire*, 1889.

Only in the middle of the nineteenth century did the cultivation of endives begin. A Belgian horticulturist named Brezier developed the vegetable accidentally through his attempts to obtain whiter chicory for salad. To prevent photosynthesis, Brezier covered the chicory with soil and planted it in an area usually reserved for the growing of mushrooms. Due to the weight of the soil, the leaves of the chicory formed in tightly overlapping layers. The vegetable, which for many years was only consumed locally, was known as Flemish chicory. It was not until 1878 that the first endives, known as *endives de Bruxelles*, appeared at Les Halles in Paris.

Serves 4

4	LARGE BELGIAN ENDIVES
	FINES HERBES VINAIGRETTE
	(RECIPE FOLLOWS)
	FRESHLY GROUND WHITE PEPPER

Wash the endives, dry with paper towels, and trim the bottoms. Cut each endive crosswise into thirds and separate any leaves that stick together. Place the cut endives in a salad bowl and pour the dressing on top. Toss the salad and correct the seasoning with a bit of freshly ground white pepper. Dress the salad just before serving, as the endives tend to wilt quickly.

FINES HERBES VINAIGRETTE
Makes ¼ cup

1	TABLESPOON RED WINE VINEGAR
	(OR VINEGAR OF CHOICE)
½	TEASPOON SALT
3	TABLESPOONS OLIVE OR VEGETABLE OIL
1	TABLESPOON CHOPPED FRESH FINES
	HERBES* OR 1 TEASPOON DRIED

*Fines herbes are a mix of such herbs as thyme, chervil, parsley, chives, tarragon, oregano, rosemary, and basil.

In a small bowl, combine the vinegar, salt, oil, and herbs. Mix well with a small wire whisk. You may also make the dressing in a cruet. Shake well before serving.

TARTE AUX ABRICOTS ET AUX PÊCHES / APRICOT-PEACH TART

ADAPTED FROM *Les 366 menus de Baron Brisse avec 1200 recettes et un calendrier nutritif,* 1875.

Serves 6–8

- 4 FIRM FRESH APRICOTS
- 2 FREESTONE PEACHES
- ½ RECIPE PÂTE BRISÉE SUCRÉE (RECIPE FOLLOWS)
- ⅔ CUP SUGAR, PLUS EXTRA FOR GLAZE
- 2 TABLESPOONS UNSALTED BUTTER
- ½ CUP APRICOT PRESERVES
- 1 TABLESPOON SUGAR

Preheat the oven to 375°F.

Drop the fruit into a large pot of boiling water for 15 seconds. Drain in a colander and allow the fruit to cool until it can be handled. Peel and halve the fruit, remove pits, and cut into ½-inch slices. Roll the *pâte brisée* out to a thickness of ¼ inch. Place the pastry in a pie plate and flute the edges if desired. Sprinkle 2–3 tablespoons of the sugar in the bottom of the pastry shell, then arrange the fruit so that the slices overlap each other slightly, forming concentric circles. Sprinkle the remaining sugar on top of the fruit and dot with the butter. Bake for 30–35 minutes on the middle rack of the oven.

When the tart is almost fully baked, make the apricot glaze. In a small saucepan, mix the apricot preserves with the sugar. Heat and stir continuously for 2–3 minutes. Strain the preserves so that only the liquid remains. Spread the glaze on the tart with a spatula. Serve the tart warm or chilled.

PÂTE BRISÉE SUCRÉE / PASTRY CRUST

Makes two 9-inch tart shells

- 1¾ CUPS SIFTED ALL-PURPOSE FLOUR
- PINCH OF SALT
- 2 TABLESPOONS SUPERFINE SUGAR
- 1½ STICKS UNSALTED BUTTER, CUT IN PIECES
- 1 EGG YOLK
- A FEW DROPS OF ICE WATER (IF NEEDED)

Blend the flour, salt, and the sugar together in a mixing bowl. Cut in the butter and continue to blend. Add the egg yolk and work in until the dough can be formed into a ball. Add a few drops of ice water if the dough is too dry. Cover the dough with plastic wrap and chill for 2 hours before rolling it out to a thickness of ¼ inch. When rolling out the dough, use either a floured surface or place it between two sheets of wax paper. Dough should be about 2 inches larger than the tart pan. Line tart pan with dough and proceed according to recipe.

[MENU № 2]

Au Restaurant Père Lathuille

Potage aux Légumes
VEGETABLE SOUP

Laitues au Jus
BRAISED LETTUCE

Poulet Sautée Père Lathuille
SAUTÉED CHICKEN PÈRE LATHUILLE

Côtes de Veau aux Girolles
VEAL CHOPS WITH MUSHROOMS

Tarte aux Poires Bourdaloue
PEAR TART WITH FRANGIPANE CREAM

Fruits de Saison
FRESH APRICOTS AND PLUMS

Vins
WINES
Sancerre (Sauvignon Blanc) / Château Trimoulet (St.-Emilion)

Café et Liqueurs
COFFEE AND LIQUEURS

THIS MENU IS INSPIRED both by Manet's suggestive double portrait set in the garden of the restaurant Père Lathuille and by the restaurant's house specialty, *Poulet Sautée Père Lathuille,* a succulent dish containing sautéed chicken, minced potatoes, and artichoke hearts topped with a light sauce of white wine, shallots, and chicken stock. The featured dessert, *Tarte aux Poires Bourdaloue* (a frangipane cream pear tart), not often prepared today, was a nineteenth-century favorite.

POTAGE AUX LÉGUMES / VEGETABLE SOUP

ADAPTED FROM LOUIS EUSTACHE AUDOT'S
La cuisinière de la campagne et de la ville, 1888.

Serves 6

- 2 TABLESPOONS UNSALTED BUTTER
- 1 SMALL ONION, SLICED
- 2 LEEKS, WHITE PART ONLY, THINLY SLICED
- 2 CLOVES GARLIC, MINCED
- 2 TURNIPS, PEELED AND DICED
- 2 SMALL POTATOES, PEELED AND DICED
- 1 CUP SHELLED FRESH PEAS
- 2 SMALL CARROTS, PEELED AND THICKLY SLICED IN ROUNDS
- 2 CABBAGE LEAVES, SHREDDED
- 2 SPRIGS FRESH PARSLEY
- 2 BAY LEAVES
- 8 CUPS VEGETABLE OR CHICKEN STOCK SALT FRESHLY GROUND WHITE PEPPER
- ¼ CUP HEAVY CREAM (OPTIONAL)

In a large saucepan, melt the butter. Add the onion, leeks, and garlic and sauté until they are soft. Do not allow the garlic to brown. Add the other vegetables and cook for about 5 minutes, stirring continuously. Add the parsley, bay leaves, and stock. Bring the soup to a boil, then reduce the heat to low. Add salt and pepper. Cover and simmer for 30 minutes.

Remove the bay leaves and purée the vegetables in a food processor. Return the mixture to the liquid and stir well. Correct the seasonings and add cream if a richer soup is desired.

LAITUES AU JUS / BRAISED LETTUCE

ADAPTED FROM GOUFFÉ'S *Le livre de cuisine*, 1867.

Dumas explains under the heading LAITUE in his *Grand dictionnaire de cuisine* that this vegetable was thus named because it was believed to increase the secretion of milk (*lait*) in nursing women.

Serves 4–8

- 4 FIRM HEADS BOSTON LETTUCE
- 5 OUNCES SMOKED HAM, FINELY CHOPPED
- 1 TABLESPOON VEGETABLE OIL
- 1 TABLESPOON UNSALTED BUTTER
- 1 CARROT, FINELY CHOPPED
- 3 SHALLOTS, FINELY CHOPPED
- 2 TEASPOONS MINCED FRESH THYME
- 1 TABLESPOON CHOPPED FRESH PARSLEY SALT
- 1 CUP CHICKEN OR VEGETABLE STOCK

Preheat the oven to 325°F.

Wash the lettuce and place the heads, whole, in a large saucepan. Cook, covered, in a small quantity of salted boiling water for 2 minutes. Drain in a colander and let cool. Squeeze out any remaining water and pat dry with a towel. Cut each head of lettuce in half, trimming the bottom if necessary.

Place half of the smoked ham in the bottom of a greased casserole, and top with the lettuce halves. In a skillet, sauté the carrot and shallots in the butter, oil, and herbs until they are tender. Top each lettuce half with the mixture and then with the remaining ham. Add the stock to the casserole and cover tightly. Bake for 1 hour. With a slotted spoon, transfer the lettuce halves to a serving dish and pour the pan juices over them. Correct the seasonings and serve hot.

POULET SAUTÉE PÈRE LATHUILLE / SAUTÉED CHICKEN PÈRE LATHUILLE

ADAPTED FROM R. COURTINE'S
Grand livre de la France à table, 1872.

Père Lathuille, the restaurant proprietor, owned a small farm just outside of Paris in the Barrière de Clichy. There, he raised the chickens to make this specialty dish of poultry, artichoke hearts, and potatoes.

Serves 4–6

    4   ARTICHOKES
    1   LEMON, CUT IN HALF
    1   LARGE FRYING CHICKEN, QUARTERED
        SALT
        FRESHLY GROUND BLACK PEPPER
    2   TABLESPOONS VEGETABLE OIL
    10 TABLESPOONS UNSALTED BUTTER
    2   TEASPOONS CHOPPED FRESH THYME
        OR 1 TEASPOON DRIED THYME
    1   BAY LEAF, CRUMBLED
    5   MEDIUM-SIZE NEW POTATOES
        PARSLEY SPRIGS (GARNISH)

For the sauce:

    1   TABLESPOON VEGETABLE OIL
    2   TABLESPOONS UNSALTED BUTTER
    ¼   CUP MINCED SHALLOTS
    ½   CUP DRY WHITE WINE
    1   CUP RICH CHICKEN STOCK
    2   TABLESPOONS TOMATO PURÉE

Preheat the oven to 375°F.

To prepare the artichoke hearts, cut off the stems of the artichokes *even* with their bases and remove all of the leaves. With a sharp knife, scoop out the chokes. Rub the hearts with a cut lemon (this will prevent them from turning gray). Drop the artichoke hearts into a pot of salted boiling water and blanch for 10 minutes. (Canned or frozen artichoke hearts may be substituted for convenience.)

Cut the chicken into 8 pieces, separating the wings from the breasts and the drumsticks from the thighs. Season with salt and pepper. Heat 1 tablespoon of the oil with 3 tablespoons of the butter in a frying pan, add the thyme and crumbled bay leaf, and lightly brown the chicken pieces on all sides. Remove to a plate and keep warm.

Cut 2 of the potatoes into thin slices. In a large skillet, sauté the potato slices in the remaining tablespoon of oil and 2 tablespoons of the butter until they are golden on both sides. Season with salt. Remove the potato slices and drain on paper towels. Add 3 more tablespoons of butter to the same skillet. Dice the other 3 potatoes and the artichoke hearts and season with salt and pepper. Sauté this mixture in the butter until it is golden.

Heat the remaining 2 tablespoons of butter and pour into a casserole. Line the bottom with the potato slices in overlapping rows. Top with half of the potato-artichoke mixture. Top the vegetables with the chicken pieces and cover with the remaining vegetables and their pan juices. Cover the casserole and bake for about 45 minutes. Unmold the casserole on a hot serving dish and garnish with parsley.

Prepare the shallot sauce by heating the oil and butter in a small saucepan and cooking the shallots until they are golden. Pour the shallot mixture into the casserole in which the chicken was cooked and scrape up pieces that have stuck to the bottom. Add the wine, chicken stock, and tomato purée and cook over high heat until the sauce is reduced and the flavor is very rich. Serve in a sauceboat.

CÔTES DE VEAU AUX GIROLLES / VEAL CHOPS WITH MUSHROOMS

ADAPTED FROM DUBOIS'S *La cuisine classique*, 1867.

In his dictionary of food, Dumas wrote that the most succulent veal was to be found in Paris. He explained this superiority as the result of two factors. First was the particular care given to the calves while they were being raised, and second was the strict observance of a law prohibiting the slaughter of these "innocent" animals before the age of six weeks.

Serves 4

- ¾ POUND MUSHROOMS (GIROLLES, PORCINI, CÈPES, MORELS, OR A COMBINATION)
- 2 TABLESPOONS VEGETABLE OIL
- 3 TABLESPOONS UNSALTED BUTTER
- ¼ CUP MINCED SHALLOTS
- 2 TABLESPOONS MINCED FRESH PARSLEY
  SALT
  FRESHLY GROUND BLACK PEPPER
- 4 LARGE VEAL CHOPS
  FLOUR
- ¾ CUP DRY WHITE WINE
- 2 TABLESPOONS BRANDY (OPTIONAL)
- ⅓ CUP CRÈME FRAÎCHE (SEE PAGE 38)

Wipe the mushrooms clean with a paper towel and slice them thick. Sauté them in a skillet with 1 tablespoon of the oil and 1 tablespoon of the butter. Add the shallots and parsley and season with salt and pepper. Simmer, covered, over gentle heat for about 10 minutes.

Season the veal chops with salt and pepper and dust with flour. In a large skillet, heat the remaining tablespoon of oil and 2 tablespoons of butter and sauté the chops until they are golden brown and thoroughly cooked. Transfer the mushrooms to a serving dish, placing them in the center. Lay the chops on top.

Prepare a sauce by adding the wine and brandy to the skillet in which the chops were cooked. Scrape the bottom of the pan to get up bits that are stuck. Bring to a boil and reduce by half. Stir in the *crème fraîche* and boil the mixture until it thickens. Pour the sauce over the meat and serve at once.

TARTE AUX POIRES BOURDALOUE / PEAR TART WITH FRANGIPANE CREAM

ADAPTED FROM THE
Nouveau manuel de la cuisine bourgeoise et économique, 1866.

Serves 6–8

- ½ RECIPE FOR **PÂTE BRISÉE SUCRÉE** (SEE PAGE 41)
- 3 CUPS FRANGIPANE CREAM (RECIPE FOLLOWS)
- 2 CUPS SUGAR, PLUS EXTRA FOR GLAZE
- 1 CUP WATER
- 1 ¼ TEASPOONS VANILLA EXTRACT
- 4 FIRM RIPE PEARS, PEELED, CORED, AND SLICED (NOT TOO THIN)
- ½ CUP APRICOT PRESERVES
- ¼ CUP FINELY CRUMBLED MACAROONS

Preheat the oven to 350°F.

[*Note:* Make the *pâte brisée sucrée* first. While it is chilling, make the frangipane cream. While the crust and cream are baking, prepare the syrup and poach the pears.]

Line a 9-inch pie plate with the *pâte brisée sucrée* and refrigerate for 1 hour. When the dough is thoroughly chilled, remove from the refrigerator and fill the pastry shell halfway with the frangipane cream. Bake the tart for ½ hour.

Meanwhile, in a saucepan over medium heat, combine the 2 cups of sugar and the water and stir well. When the sugar has dissolved, add the vanilla and raise the heat to high. Bring the syrup to a boil and keep at the boiling point, without stirring, for 10 minutes. Use immediately or store in a covered jar at room temperature.

Poach the pear slices, a few at a time, in the vanilla syrup over gentle heat for 3–5 minutes, or until they are tender but firm when pricked with a fork. Drain the pears and allow to cool.

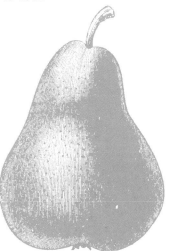

When the tart is baked and has cooled, put the remaining cream into it. Arrange the pear slices on top of the cream in overlapping rows.

To make the glaze, heat the apricot preserves in a small saucepan with 1 tablespoon of sugar. When the preserves become syrupy, remove from the heat and strain.

With a spatula, spread the glaze on top of the pears. Top with macaroon crumbs and allow to cool before serving.

FRANGIPANE CREAM

8	EGG YOLKS
¾	CUPS SUGAR
¼	CUP UNSALTED BUTTER, SOFTENED
	PINCH OF SALT
¾	CUP SIFTED ALL-PURPOSE FLOUR (OR MORE, IF NECESSARY)
4	CUPS MILK, BOILED
½	CUP FINELY CRUMBLED MACAROONS
2	TEASPOONS VANILLA EXTRACT

In a heavy-bottomed saucepan, combine the egg yolks and sugar and beat with a wire whisk. When the mixture is very smooth, add the butter, salt, and flour. Gradually stir in the boiling milk and continue stirring until the mixture is very smooth. Over low heat, bring the mixture to a boil, stirring constantly with a whisk. Boil slowly for several minutes, being careful that the bottom does not burn. Scrape the bottom while stirring to prevent sticking. Remove from the heat and continue to stir for 2–3 minutes.

Place the finely crumbled macaroons in a mixing bowl and pour the mixture on top, stirring continuously. Add the vanilla and mix well. If you're not using the cream right away, cover and refrigerate.

[MENU № 3]

Le Déjeuner sur l'Herbe

Radis Roses et Beurre
RED RADISHES AND BUTTER

Olives Vertes et Noires
GREEN AND BLACK OLIVES

Omelette aux Pointes d'Asperges
ASPARAGUS-TIP OMELETTE

Tomates Farcies au Maigre
STUFFED TOMATOES

Cailles aux Raisins
ROAST QUAIL WITH GRAPES

Fromages Assortis
ASSORTED CHEESES: CAMEMBERT AND GRUYÈRE

Tarte aux Cerises
CHERRY TART

Vins
WINES
Saint-Véran (Mâconnais) / Château Beauregard (Pommard)

UNDOUBTEDLY THE MOST PROVOCATIVE portrait of a picnic party in the history of art, Manet's painting is the inspiration for this light, yet delectable menu. The featured foods, *Omelette aux Pointes d'Asperges*, *Tomates Farcies au Maigre*, and *Cailles aux Raisins*, make wonderful finger food. Equally delicious whether eaten at home, hot from the oven, or outdoors, unpacked from a picnic basket, these dishes remain classics today and are still widely served throughout France.

RADIS ROSES ET BEURRE /
RED RADISHES AND BUTTER
ADAPTED FROM AUDOT'S
La cuisinière de la campagne et de la ville, 1857.

Radishes served with butter were a popular hors d'oeuvre in France in the nineteenth century, and most cookbooks of the time included directions for their use. French radishes tend to be a lighter shade of pink, somewhat longer, and less round than their American counterparts. While many Americans shun the radish, often finding its taste too sharp, radishes are still quite popular in France today and are readily found in open-air vegetable markets. Some farmers in this country have begun to plant the French radishes, which are known as French Breakfast radishes.

Serves 4

1 BUNCH FRESH RED RADISHES WITH TOPS
1 BAGUETTE OR OTHER FRENCH-TYPE BREAD
UNSALTED BUTTER
SALT

Remove the stems and tips from the radishes and discard. Wash the radishes well under running water and drain in a colander. Cut the baguette into slices and butter the rounds. Place on a tray with the radishes. Serve with salt.

OLIVES VERTES ET NOIRES /
GREEN AND BLACK OLIVES
ADAPTED FROM AUDOT'S
La cuisinière de la campagne et de la ville, 1857.

You can either buy these wonderfully flavorful hors d'oeuvre olives at a specialty store or make them at home, allowing a day or two for the olives to marinate in the oil and spices.

GREEN OLIVES
Serves 4

1 CUP GREEN OLIVES WITH PITS,
DRAINED WELL
¼ CUP RED WINE OR BALSAMIC VINEGAR
¼ CUP OLIVE OIL
1 CLOVE GARLIC, MINCED
1 SHALLOT, MINCED
2 PINCHES OF SALT
½ TEASPOON BLACK PEPPERCORNS

On a cutting board, crush the olives slightly with the side of a knife until the pits show. Transfer the olives to a small bowl and combine with the other ingredients. Mix well and allow to marinate overnight at room temperature.

BLACK OLIVES

Serves 4

1 CUP BLACK OLIVES WITH PITS, DRAINED WELL
¼ CUP OLIVE OIL (PREFERABLY EXTRA VIRGIN)
1 CLOVE GARLIC, CRUSHED
2 PINCHES OF SALT
PINCH OF HOT RED PEPPER FLAKES
1 ½ TEASPOONS HERBES DE PROVENCE (AVAILABLE IN SPECIALTY STORES AND SOME SUPERMARKETS)

On a cutting board, crush the olives slightly until the pits show. Transfer the olives to a small bowl and combine with other ingredients. Mix well and allow to marinate overnight at room temperature.

OMELETTE AUX POINTES D'ASPERGES / ASPARAGUS-TIP OMELETTE

ADAPTED FROM DUBOIS'S *La cuisine classique*, 1867.

Egg dishes were extremely popular in nineteenth-century French cuisine, and a great variety of omelettes were served both *salé* (savory) and *sucré* (sweet). The recipe index of Dubois's celebrated cookbook lists twenty-seven entries under the heading OMELETTE. These include anchovy, onion, cheese, potato, ham, bacon, mixed vegetable, tuna, tomato, jelly, rum, and sugar omelettes.

Serves 2

1 CUP ASPARAGUS TIPS, CHOPPED
4 TABLESPOONS UNSALTED BUTTER
SALT
FRESHLY GROUND WHITE PEPPER
6 EGGS
1 TABLESPOON WATER OR MILK
1 SPRIG WATERCRESS (GARNISH)

Sauté the asparagus tips in 2 tablespoons of the butter for 3–5 minutes. Be sure not to overcook; the tips should stay firm. Season with a little salt and pepper and set aside. In a bowl, beat the eggs just until they are blended. Do not overbeat. Add salt, pepper, and the water. Heat the remaining butter in a skillet or omelette pan. (If your omelette pan is too small, make two individual omelettes.) When the butter begins to foam and then subsides, the pan is hot enough. Pour in the egg mixture and stir immediately, using a fork. The heat should be at medium-high.

Raise and lower the pan to control the heat. When the omelette has set a little, spoon the asparagus filling across the middle. As the omelette continues to cook, run the fork around the edges to be sure the eggs are not sticking to the bottom or sides of the skillet. Roll up the omelette in the following manner: gripping the handle palm side up and raising it, fold the omelette over in thirds by bringing the outside edge to the inside, then slide the omelette onto a warm serving dish. Garnish with watercress.

TOMATES FARCIES AU MAIGRE / STUFFED TOMATOES

ADAPTED FROM DUBOIS's *La cuisine classique*, 1867.

Stuffed vegetables, especially onions, tomatoes, and eggplants were very popular in French cookery during the last century. Because these dishes were frequently made with sausage or another kind of meat, special preparations such as the one that follows were practical on lean or fast days—hence the *au maigre*, or meatless, distinction.

Serves 4

- 4 LARGE RIPE TOMATOES
-   SALT
-   FRESHLY GROUND WHITE PEPPER
- 3 CUPS SOFT WHITE BREAD CRUMBS (USE DAY-OLD BREAD)
- ½ CUP MILK
- 2 EGGS, LIGHTLY BEATEN
- 1 TABLESPOON EACH MINCED FRESH BASIL, CHIVES, PARSLEY, AND OREGANO
- 1 CLOVE GARLIC, MINCED
- 3 SHALLOTS, MINCED
- 4 TABLESPOONS GRUYÈRE OR SWISS-TYPE CHEESE, GRATED
- 2 TABLESPOONS DRY UNSEASONED BREAD CRUMBS
- 2 TABLESPOONS OLIVE OIL

Preheat the oven to 300°F.

Wash the tomatoes and pat dry. Cut a thin slice from the stem portion of each tomato and scoop out the pulp. Season the insides with salt and pepper. To prepare the stuffing, place the soft bread crumbs in a bowl, add the milk, and mix with a fork. Stir in the eggs. Add the herbs, garlic, and shallots. Season with a little salt and pepper.

Drain the tomatoes before stuffing them. Place the tomatoes in a greased baking dish. Fill them with the stuffing and top with the grated cheese and dry bread crumbs. Drizzle with a little olive oil and bake for 30–35 minutes. Transfer to a heated serving dish and serve very hot.

CAILLES AUX RAISINS / ROAST QUAIL WITH GRAPES

ADAPTED FROM DUBOIS's *La cuisine classique*, 1867.

Before the French Revolution, the eating of game, pheasant, hare, venison, partridge, wild duck, or quail was a privilege enjoyed only by the noble class. As social relations were reorganized during the nineteenth century, a vast array of dishes began to appear on restaurant tables and in bourgeois households, where they had never before been seen. In the 1867 edition of Dubois's cookbook, ten recipes are given for preparing quail, either roasted, braised, *au gratin*, with lard, or with bay leaves.

Serves 2

- 4 QUAIL
- 6 TABLESPOONS UNSALTED BUTTER, SOFTENED
-   SALT
-   FRESHLY GROUND WHITE PEPPER
- 20 SEEDLESS GREEN GRAPES, PEELED AND HALVED
- ½ CUP CHICKEN STOCK, HEATED

Preheat the oven to 450°F.

Wash and pat dry each quail. Melt the butter in an ovenproof casserole and season quail with salt and pepper before browning quickly on all sides. Place the casserole in a hot oven for about 10 minutes. Remove from the oven and set casserole on stove top. Add the grapes and heated stock, cover and bring to a boil.

Serve from the casserole or arrange the grapes around the quail on individual plates.

TARTE AUX CERISES / CHERRY TART

ADAPTED FROM *Les 366 menus de Baron Brisse*
avec 1200 recettes et un calendrier nutritif, 1875.

Serves 6–8

- ½ RECIPE **PÂTE BRISÉE SUCRÉE**
  (SEE PAGE 41)
- ½ CUP SUPERFINE SUGAR (USE LESS IF
  CHERRIES ARE VERY SWEET)
- 2 CUPS FRESH CHERRIES, PITTED
- 2 CUPS CRÈME PÂTISSIÈRE (RECIPE FOLLOWS)
- ½ CUP CHERRY OR RED CURRANT JELLY

Preheat the oven to 350°F.

Line a 9-inch tart pan with the pastry. Chill thoroughly for 30 minutes. Sprinkle the pastry with some of the sugar and lay the cherries in it. Sprinkle the remaining sugar on top of the fruit. Pour the *crème pâtissière* over the fruit and bake on the lowest rack of the oven for about 45 minutes. Remove from oven and while tart is cooling, make the glaze.

Melt the jelly in a small saucepan over medium heat. When it is syrupy, remove from the heat and spread lightly on top of the *crème pâtissière* with a spatula. Serve the tart warm or at room temperature.

CRÈME PÂTISSIÈRE

Makes about 2½ cups

- ¾ CUP SUGAR
- 5 EGG YOLKS
- ¾ CUP SIFTED ALL-PURPOSE FLOUR
- 2 WHOLE EGGS
- 2 CUPS MILK
- 2 TEASPOONS VANILLA EXTRACT
- 2 TABLESPOONS KIRSCH
- 1 TABLESPOON UNSALTED BUTTER (OPTIONAL)

[*Note:* Do not use aluminum pans to make the cream because the metal can cause the mixture to discolor.]

Off the heat in a heavy-bottomed saucepan, combine the sugar and egg yolks, adding 1 yolk at a time to the sugar. Using a wooden spoon, beat the mixture well after each addition until the sugar has completely absorbed the egg yolks. Add the flour and 1 whole egg. Beat mixture smooth before adding the second whole egg.

In another saucepan, heat the milk to the boiling point. Warm the contents of the first saucepan and then add the boiling liquid. Continue cooking over low heat, stirring constantly and scraping the bottom and sides of the pan. When the mixture starts to bubble, cook for a few minutes more. Pour the mixture into a large mixing bowl to cool. Add the vanilla and kirsch. If not using immediately, butter the top surface of the cream to prevent a skin from forming. The cream keeps well when refrigerated; it may also be frozen.

A Light Supper at the Folies-Bergère

Consommé Printanier
SPRINGTIME CONSOMMÉ

Saumon Fumé
SMOKED SALMON

Blinis à la Russe
BLINI WITH CAVIAR

Huîtres à la Coquille
OYSTERS ON THE HALF SHELL

Baba au Rhum
RUM CAKE

Poires Josette
POACHED PEARS WITH ICE CREAM

Vins
WINES
Pouilly-Fuissé / Vodka / Champagne Bollinger

Café et Liqueurs
COFFEE AND LIQUEURS

A TRIBUTE TO LÉON SARI, the creative spirit behind the Folies-Bergère, this late-night menu is composed of mouthwatering dishes and drinks designed to lift the spirits. *Saumon Fumé* and *Huîtres à la Coquille* were popular delicacies in nineteenth-century France. *Poires Josette*, a poached pear and ice cream confection, was a specialty dessert of Drouant, one of Paris's better restaurants—an establishment Manet would have had occasion to frequent.

CONSOMMÉ PRINTANIER / SPRINGTIME CONSOMMÉ

ADAPTED FROM AUDOT'S
La cuisinière de la campagne et de la ville, 1857.

Serves 4

½	CUP DICED BABY CARROTS
½	CUP DICED TURNIPS
½	CUP SHELLED FRESH PEAS
½	CUP THINLY SLICED LEEKS
5	CUPS BEEF OR CHICKEN STOCK
½	CUP WATERCRESS, LEAVES ONLY
	FRESHLY GROUND WHITE PEPPER (OPTIONAL)

In a pot of salted boiling water, cook the carrots, turnips, peas, and leeks for about 5 minutes and drain. In another pot, heat the stock. When it is boiling, add the vegetables and cook until tender but still slightly firm. Just before serving, toss in the watercress leaves. Season with fresh pepper if desired.

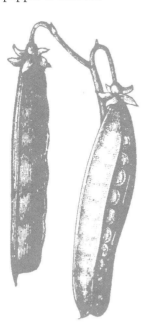

SAUMON FUMÉ / SMOKED SALMON

ADAPTED FROM THE
Nouveau manuel de la cuisine bourgeoise et économique, 1866.

In nineteenth-century France, smoked salmon was most frequently served on thin, toasted rounds of *pain de mie* (soft white bread). The bread was either buttered or spread with *beurre d'anchois* (anchovy butter), and then topped with a slice of salmon. If you wish to be faithful to the nineteenth century, use white rather than dark bread.

Serves 4

	BREAD OF CHOICE
	UNSALTED BUTTER, SOFTENED
¼	POUND SMOKED SALMON
1	LEMON, CUT INTO WEDGES
	FRESHLY GROUND BLACK PEPPER (OPTIONAL)
	FRESH DILL, CHOPPED (OPTIONAL)

Lightly toast the bread, then butter and cut into halves or quarters, depending on the size of the serving you want. Top with a thin slice of salmon and serve with lemon, seasoned with pepper and dill, or plain (*au nature*). The salmon may also be served with the blini (see recipe on page 62).

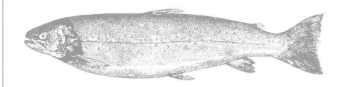

BLINIS À LA RUSSE / BLINI WITH CAVIAR
ADAPTED FROM AUDOT'S
La cuisinière de la campagne et de la ville, 1857.

Dating back to the pre–Christian era, blini are one of the most ancient Slavic foods. Toward the end of the nineteenth century, they grew in popularity as a delicacy in France. Because it was customary to serve them with caviar, they were named *Blinis à la Russe*—Blini Russian Style. Because of their Russian origin, blini should be served with vodka. Contrary to popular belief, these gourmet "pancakes" are not traditionally made from buckwheat flour. Here is a classic recipe for this centuries-old delight:

Makes 2½ dozen. Serves 8–10 as an appetizer.

- 4 CUPS MILK
- 4 TEASPOONS SUGAR
- 2 TABLESPOONS ACTIVE DRY YEAST (2 PACKAGES)
- 3 CUPS SIFTED ALL-PURPOSE FLOUR
- 1 TEASPOON SALT
- 2 TABLESPOONS VEGETABLE OIL, PLUS OIL FOR COOKING
- 3 TABLESPOONS UNSALTED BUTTER, MELTED
- 4 EGGS, SEPARATED

In a small saucepan, scald 3 cups of the milk over gentle heat. Transfer to a large mixing bowl and cool to lukewarm. Stir in 1 teaspoon of the sugar and all of the yeast and let stand until the mixture is foamy. Whisk in half of the flour until the batter is smooth. Cover the bowl with a towel and place in a warm spot about 1 hour or until the dough has doubled in bulk.

Add the remaining flour, the salt, 2 tablespoons oil, the butter, and the remaining sugar. Mix well and allow to rise, covered, until doubled in bulk.

In a small saucepan, bring the remaining 1 cup of milk just to the boiling point. Allow to cool for several minutes, then add to the batter, beating well. Beat the egg yolks and add.

In a separate bowl, beat the egg whites until they form stiff peaks and then fold into the batter. Allow to rise again, covered, in a warm place, 30–40 minutes.

Using a nonstick skillet or preferably a crêpe pan, grease the bottom with vegetable oil and heat for 60 seconds. (The traditional way to grease a pan for blini is to dip a cut potato in oil and rub the bottom of the skillet. In this way, just the right amount of oil is applied to the pan each time.) Pour about ¼ cup of the batter into the pan and tilt the skillet so that the batter covers the whole surface in a fine layer. Cook about 60 seconds, or until the underside is golden. Flip the blin and cook for another 30 seconds. (Taste the first blin to see if any last-minute adjustments are in order. If necessary, add more salt, sugar, flour, or milk if proportions seem off in any way.)

Repeat the process with the rest of the batter, being sure to grease the pan before making each blin. To keep the blini hot as you prepare them, set in a deep ovenproof serving dish and keep covered with aluminum foil in a warm (275°F) oven. Serve with caviar, sour cream, and/or smoked salmon.

HUÎTRES À LA COQUILLE / OYSTERS ON THE HALF SHELL
ADAPTED FROM AUDOT'S
La cuisinière de la campagne et de la ville, 1857.

From the middle of the nineteenth century onward, oyster consumption in Paris was on the rise. In 1846 as many as 72 million oysters were consumed in France's capital, that figure representing more than 6 dozen oysters per person per year. If, however, out of every million, only 200 to 250 thousand persons had the economic means to enjoy oysters, the figure is an amazing 25 dozen oysters per person. (For oyster consumption, see Jean-Paul Aron's *Le mangeur du XIXième siècle.*)

Serves 4

    24   OYSTERS IN THEIR SHELLS
     1   LEMON, CUT INTO WEDGES
         SHALLOT SAUCE (RECIPE FOLLOWS)

Open the oysters and arrange on a bed of ice. Squeeze a few drops of lemon juice over each one or a few drops of the shallot sauce.

VINAIGRE À L'ECHALOTE / SHALLOT SAUCE
Makes about ¼ cup

    ¼   CUP RED WINE VINEGAR
    2   SHALLOTS, FINELY MINCED
    ¼   TEASPOON FRESHLY GROUND BLACK
        OR WHITE PEPPER

In a small bowl, combine all the ingredients. Mix well and spoon a little of the sauce over each oyster.

BABA AU RHUM / RUM CAKE
ADAPTED FROM AUDOT'S
La cuisinière de la campagne et de la ville, 1857.

In his *Grand dictionnaire de cuisine,* Dumas wrote of this noble cake: "The baba is a cake of Polish origin, which should always be served in a size large enough to act as an impressive centerpiece, usually the main dish in a course, and remain for several days on the sideboard as a standby." Dumas stated that when babas were served in royal households, they were always accompanied by a sauceboat containing sweet Malaga wine. The great French writer remarked that in Paris one sometimes saw babas "which have been made in small molds, but these dry out too easily to permit approval of this economical method, which in any case is used only by commercial pastry cooks." For the home cook, Dumas recommended the recipe for baba that appears in Audot's *La cuisinière de la campagne et de la ville.*

Serves 10 or more

    2   TABLESPOONS ACTIVE DRY YEAST
        (2 PACKAGES)
    ¾   CUP LUKEWARM WATER
    ¼   CUP GRANULATED SUGAR
    ½   CUP CONFECTIONERS' SUGAR
    6   EGGS, BEATEN
    ¾   CUP (1 ½ STICKS) UNSALTED BUTTER,
        SOFTENED
    4   CUPS ALL-PURPOSE FLOUR (MORE WILL BE
        ADDED AS DOUGH IS KNEADED)
    ½   CUP CURRANTS OR RAISINS, SOAKED IN
        RUM OVERNIGHT

For the rum sauce:

    1   CUP GRANULATED SUGAR (MORE IF
        A HEAVIER SYRUP IS DESIRED)
    2   CUPS WATER
    ¾   CUP DARK RUM

In a large mixing bowl, dissolve the yeast in ¼ cup of the warm water with 1 teaspoon of the granulated sugar. The mixture will foam. Allow to stand about 5 minutes. Add the remaining water, sugar, the confectioners' sugar, and eggs and beat well until the mixture is smooth. Add the butter and beat until smooth.

Add the flour, 1 cup at a time, stirring after each addition until the flour has been incorporated. Turn out the dough onto a floured surface and knead until smooth and elastic. Add as much flour as necessary to prevent sticking. Drain the currants or raisins well and incorporate them into dough. Generously grease a large tube pan and lay in the dough. Cover with a dish towel and let rise for an hour or so in a warm place free of drafts.

Preheat the oven to 375°F. Bake the baba for about 45 minutes, until it is golden brown. Invert and let cool on a rack.

Meanwhile, prepare the rum sauce. In a small saucepan, heat the sugar and water. Stir well and bring to a boil. Add the rum and return to a boil. Remove from the heat. When the baba has cooled, set on a serving dish, prick the top and sides, and pour the rum sauce over it. Allow to sit for at least 30 minutes before serving. (If serving the following day, wrap the baba well and allow to remain at room temperature.)

POIRES JOSETTE /
POACHED PEARS WITH ICE CREAM
ADAPTED FROM *Almanach des ménagères et gastronomes*, C. 1878.

This elegant and scrumptious dessert was a specialty of the restaurant Drouant, one of Paris's better addresses in the late nineteenth century. Monet was a devotee of the restaurant and would dine there with Alice Hoschedé, his second wife, on their frequent excursions to Paris for theater, concerts, or other cultural events.

Serves 4

- 2 CUPS SUGAR
- 1 CUP WATER
- 1 ¼ TEASPOONS VANILLA EXTRACT
- 3 FIRM RIPE PEARS
- 1 PINT VANILLA ICE CREAM
  CRÈME CHANTILLY (RECIPE FOLLOWS)
  FRESH MINT SPRIGS (GARNISH)

Prepare the syrup. In a saucepan over medium heat, combine the sugar and water and stir well. When the sugar has dissolved add the vanilla extract and raise the heat to high. Bring the syrup to a boil and keep at the boiling point, without stirring for 10 minutes. Use immediately or store in a covered jar at room temperature.

Peel, core, and halve each pear. Bring the syrup to a boil, drop in the pear halves, and poach for 5–8 minutes, or until tender but firm. Remove the pears from the syrup with a slotted spoon and allow to cool completely. Refrigerate for several hours.

On each of 4 plates, place a pear half and fill the center with ice cream. Top with *crème Chantilly* and garnish with a sprig of fresh mint.

CRÈME CHANTILLY
- 1 CUP (½ PINT) HEAVY CREAM, WELL CHILLED
- ¼ CUP SUPERFINE SUGAR
- ¾ TEASPOON VANILLA EXTRACT

In a chilled bowl, whip the cream with a wire whisk or hand mixer. Add half of the sugar and the vanilla, and continue to whip, gradually adding the rest of the sugar. When soft peaks begin to form when the beater is lifted, the cream is ready. Refrigerate if not using immediately.

[Menu № 5]

A Luncheon at La Grenouillère

Potage aux Tomates
Tomato Soup

Croquettes de Pommes de Terre
Potato Croquettes

Chou-fleur Sauté au Beurre
Cauliflower Sautéed in Butter

Fritures de Seine
Fried Fish Seine Style

Côtes de Porc Grillés aux Herbes
Grilled Pork Chops with Herbs

Crème au Citron
Lemon Custard

Tarte aux Mirabelles
Yellow Plum Tart

Vins
Wines
Pouilly-Fumé / Domaine Tempier (Bandol)

Café et Liqueurs
Coffee and Liqueurs

Set at La Grenouillère, the fabled floating dining establishment frequented and painted by the Impressionists and their circle, this menu features the typical fare at the many informal eateries that sprang up along the Seine on the outskirts of Paris. The *Fritures de Seine* are mentioned in Guy de Maupassant's short story "Une partie de campagne," and the *Croquettes de Pommes de Terre*, a natural accompaniment to the fish, utilize the most common nineteenth-century vegetable, the potato.

POTAGE AUX TOMATES / TOMATO SOUP
ADAPTED FROM THE
Nouveau manuel de la cuisine bourgeoise et économique, 1866.

Serves 4–6

- 1 TABLESPOON VEGETABLE OR OLIVE OIL (NOT EXTRA VIRGIN)
- 1 LARGE ONION, FINELY CHOPPED
- 1 CLOVE GARLIC, MINCED
- 8 LARGE RIPE TOMATOES, SEEDED AND CHOPPED
- 4½ CUPS CHICKEN STOCK
- 1 TABLESPOON SHERRY (OPTIONAL)
- 3 TABLESPOONS VERY FINE VERMICELLI
- 2 TABLESPOONS CHOPPED FRESH CHERVIL
  SALT
  FRESHLY GROUND WHITE PEPPER

Heat the oil in a skillet and sauté the onion until transparent. Add the garlic and cook until soft but do not allow to brown. Place the tomatoes in a large saucepan containing the heated chicken stock. Add the sherry if using. Cook the tomatoes for 20–25 minutes over low heat and then purée in a food processor, along with the onion and garlic. Pour the purée back into the stock and mix well. Season with salt and pepper. Over medium heat, bring the mixture to a boil, add the vermicelli, and reduce the heat. Remove from the heat when vermicelli are *al dente*. Serve with chervil sprinkled on top.

CROQUETTES DE POMMES DE TERRE / POTATO CROQUETTES
ADAPTED FROM DUBOIS's *La cuisine classique, 1867.*

Potatoes were an important part of the diet of the French during the last century and are still widely eaten today. The recipe indexes of midcentury cookbooks reveal the popularity of the potato. In Dubois's *La cuisine classique*, forty-four recipes appear under the heading POMMES DE TERRE.

Serves 4

- 1 POUND POTATOES (IDAHO OR RUSSET)
- 1 TABLESPOON UNSALTED BUTTER
- 1 WHOLE EGG
- 1 EGG YOLK
- ¾ TEASPOON SALT
  FRESHLY GROUND WHITE PEPPER
  FRESHLY GRATED NUTMEG
- ½ CUP DRY BREADCRUMBS
  VEGETABLE OIL FOR FRYING
- 1 TABLESPOON CHOPPED FRESH PARSLEY (OPTIONAL)

Cut the peeled potatoes into quarters and place them in a pot of salted water. Boil until soft when pierced with a fork and drain well before mashing. Add the butter, eggs and seasonings (to taste) and mix well with a wooden spoon. Continue to blend the mixture until smooth. Refrigerate for two hours so that the mixture can stiffen.

Heat the oil in a skillet. Form the potato mixture into small balls 1-inch in diameter by rolling each spoonful in the palm of your hand. Coat the croquettes in the breadcrumbs and drop them into the hot oil. When the croquettes are a rich golden color all over, remove them with a slotted spoon and drain on paper towels. Serve hot. Garnish with parsley if desired.

CHOU-FLEUR SAUTÉ AU BEURRE / CAULIFLOWER SAUTÉED IN BUTTER

ADAPTED FROM AUDOT'S
La cuisinière de la campagne et de la ville, 1857.

Serves 4–6

 1   LARGE UNBLEMISHED HEAD CAULIFLOWER
 6   TABLESPOONS UNSALTED BUTTER
     SALT
     FRESHLY GROUND WHITE PEPPER
 2½ TABLESPOONS MINCED FINES HERBES
     (SEE NOTE ON PAGE 40)

Cut flowerets from the head of cauliflower and place in a large kettle of generously salted boiling water. Boil for 5–10 minutes, or until they are about three-fourths cooked. The stems should be slightly firm when pricked with a fork. (You may steam them if you prefer.)

Melt the butter in a large skillet, add the flowerets, and cook until golden, turning frequently. Transfer to a hot serving dish and pour the pan juices over the flowerets. Season with salt and pepper. Sprinkle with the chopped herbs and serve.

FRITURES DE SEINE / FRIED FISH SEINE STYLE

ADAPTED FROM AUDOT'S
La cuisinière de la campagne et de la ville, 1857.

This recipe pays homage to the writer Guy de Maupassant, who must surely have eaten his fill of *fritures* at the many *gargotes* ("greasy spoons") that dotted the banks of the Seine, where he loved to go boating.

Serves 4

 3   POUNDS SMALL FRESHWATER FISH OR
     2 POUNDS FILLETS
     MILK
     ALL-PURPOSE FLOUR
     VEGETABLE OIL FOR FRYING
     SALT
     FRESHLY GROUND BLACK PEPPER
     SEVERAL LEMONS, CUT IN WEDGES
     PARSLEY SPRIGS (GARNISH)

If using small fish, leave them whole. If using fillets, cut them into 2- to 3-inch pieces. Dip the fish in a bowl of cold milk and soak for 5–10 minutes. Drain and coat with flour. In a large skillet, heat the oil to 375°F. (Use a frying thermometer to gauge the temperature.) Add the fish and fry until golden on both sides. Drain on paper towels and transfer to a serving dish lined with a napkin to absorb excess oil. Season with salt and pepper and serve at once with lemon wedges and parsley.

CÔTES DE PORC GRILLÉS AUX HERBES / GRILLED PORK CHOPS WITH HERBS

ADAPTED FROM *Les 366 menus de Baron Brisse avec 1200 recettes et un calendrier nutritif*, 1875.

During the first quarter of the nineteenth century in Paris, pork consumption was very high, surpassing that of beef and veal, although mutton consumption exceeded it by almost five times. Pork continues to play a significant role in the diet of the French today. The popularity of *charcuterie* (sausages, terrines, rillettes, hams, and pâtés) attests to this fact.

Serves 4

- 4 THICK LOIN PORK CHOPS
- ¾ CUP OLIVE OIL
- 1 TABLESPOON EACH MINCED FRESH SAGE, ROSEMARY, THYME, AND CHIVES
- 2 CLOVES GARLIC, MINCED
   SALT
   FRESHLY GROUND BLACK PEPPER
   FRESH ROSEMARY SPRIGS (GARNISH)

Prepare a marinade for the chops by mixing the oil, minced herbs, and garlic in a bowl. Allow the meat to marinate overnight in the refrigerator. When ready to cook the chops, drain them and season with salt and pepper. Broil under medium heat 8–10 minutes on each side, or to the desired degree of doneness. Serve on a platter garnished with rosemary sprigs.

CRÈME AU CITRON / LEMON CUSTARD

ADAPTED FROM MÉLANIE CARÊME's *Le parfait Cordon Bleu*, C. 1870.

Serves 4–6

- 2 CUPS HEAVY CREAM OR HALF-AND-HALF
- 2 CUPS MILK
- ½ CUP SUPERFINE SUGAR
- 2 TEASPOONS LEMON EXTRACT
- 6 EGG YOLKS, BEATEN WELL

In a double boiler, heat the cream, milk, sugar, and lemon extract. When the mixture is very hot and almost at a boil, reduce the heat and gradually add the egg yolks, whisking constantly. Continue to cook, stirring constantly, for about 20 minutes, making sure the mixture does not come to a boil. When it has thickened to a custard, remove from the heat and transfer to individual soufflé or mousse dishes. Cool before serving alone or with *Sablé* cookies (see page 113).

TARTE AUX MIRABELLES /
YELLOW PLUM TART

ADAPTED FROM GOUFFÉ'S *Le livre de cuisine*, 1867.

"Plums," wrote Dumas in the *Grand dictionnaire de cuisine*, "were brought from Syria and Damascus by the Crusades, and their different names, as one would suppose, have special significance . . . those called Mirabelle were brought first to Provence and then to Lorraine by King René. . . . Plums are an excellent fruit, very sweet, and very nutritious."

Serves 6–8

- ½ RECIPE **PÂTE BRISÉE SUCRÉE** (SEE PAGE 41)
- ⅔ CUP SUPERFINE SUGAR
- 10 YELLOW OR GREEN GAGE PLUMS, HALVED AND PITTED
- 2 TABLESPOONS UNSALTED BUTTER, CUT IN PIECES
  GROUND CINNAMON (OPTIONAL)
- ½ CUP OF APRICOT PRESERVES
- 1 TABLESPOON SUGAR

Line a 9-inch tart pan with the pastry and refrigerate until thoroughly chilled. Preheat the oven to 375°F.

Sprinkle 3 tablespoons of the sugar in the bottom of the pastry shell. Place the plum halves (cut side up) closely together in the pie shell. Sprinkle the rest of the sugar on top of the fruit and dot with the butter. Add cinnamon, if using.

Bake for 35–45 minutes or until the fruit juices are syrupy. While the pie is baking, make the apricot glaze.

In a small saucepan, mix the apricot preserves with the sugar. Heat and stir continuously for 2–3 minutes. Strain the preserves so that only the liquid remains.

When the tart is fully cooked, remove from oven and spread the warm glaze over the plums in an even layer. Serve slightly warm or at room temperature.

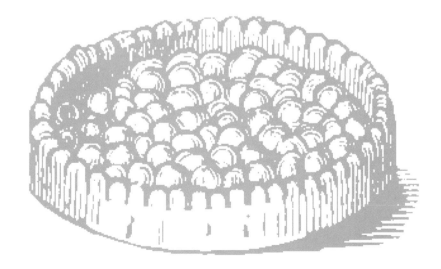

Picnic of the Cherry Pickers

Cornichons au Vinaigre
PICKLED CUCUMBERS

Saucissons Secs
HARD SAUSAGE

Quiche au Roquefort
ROQUEFORT CHEESE QUICHE

Oignons Farcis
STUFFED ONIONS

Haricots Verts en Salade
STRING BEAN SALAD

Poulet Rôti au Romarin
ROSEMARY ROAST CHICKEN

Clafouti aux Cerises
CHERRY FLAN

Fruits de Saison
FRESH GRAPES AND PEACHES

Vins
WINES
Gigondas (Vaucluse) / Hermitage Blanc

ORGANIZED AROUND THE TWIN PLEASURES of picnicking and cherry picking in an orchard, this menu features the produce of summer-tender string beans, or the more slender French green beans, and ruby-red cherries. Included are a few simple picnic favorites such as *cornichons* and *saucissons*, a traditional combination, along with quiche and cold roast chicken. *Clafouti aux Cerises* is a delicious, classic country dessert and a wonderful way to make use of fresh cherries.

CORNICHONS AU VINAIGRE / PICKLED CUCUMBERS

While it isn't difficult to make cornichons at home, it's difficult to find the tiny, delicate pickling cucumbers required to make them. I recommend buying a jar of imported cornichons. Many supermarkets, in addition to specialty food stores, now stock them.

SAUCISSONS SECS / HARD SAUSAGE

From Dubois's *La cuisine classique*, 1867.

The best hard sausages come from a *charcuterie,* where a variety of pork products are sold. In the nineteenth century, hard sausages from Lyons, Arles, Italy, and Germany were frequently served as hors d'oeuvres. In Gouffé's *Le livre de cuisine*, the great chef instructs that the sausage be cut in slices ½ centimeter thick (about ¼ inch) and that the rounds be peeled before serving.

    1   SAUCISSON À L'AIL (GARLIC SAUSAGE)
    1   SAUCISSON SEC AU POIVRE VERT
        (GREEN PEPPERCORN SAUSAGE)
    1   BAGUETTE
        UNSALTED BUTTER (OPTIONAL)

Cut each sausage into thin rounds, remove the skins, and serve with slices of bread, with or without butter.

QUICHE AU ROQUEFORT / ROQUEFORT CHEESE QUICHE

Adapted from Dubois's *La cuisine classique*, 1867.

Roquefort, a blue cheese from the Aveyron in south central France, was already popular at the beginning of the nineteenth century. In *Le ventre de Paris*, Zola describes the cheeses for sale—Brie, Port-Salut, Parmesan, Cantal, chèvre, and Roquefort—at a *fromagerie* at Les Halles. For the great French writer, the Roqueforts had a princely air with their rich surfaces, marbled in blue and yellow—*"veinées de bleu et de jaune."*

Serves 4–6

    1   RECIPE PÂTE BRISÉE (RECIPE FOLLOWS)
    1 ¼   CUPS HEAVY CREAM (USE LIGHT CREAM OR
          HALF-AND-HALF, IF DESIRED)
    4   EGGS
    ½   CUP CRUMBLED ROQUEFORT CHEESE
          FRESHLY GROUND WHITE PEPPER
    1   TEASPOON FINELY MINCED CHIVES
          (OPTIONAL)

Preheat the oven to 400°F.

Line an 8- or 9-inch tart pan with the *pâte brisée.* Place a sheet of aluminum foil on top and fill with dried peas or rice to prevent the pastry shell from puffing up. Bake for 10 minutes, remove from the oven, and remove the foil.

Lower the oven temperature to 350°F. In a mixing bowl, blend the cream, eggs, and cheese. Beat until the mixture is smooth and creamy. Season with pepper. Pour the mixture into the partially baked pastry shell, being careful not to overfill it. Sprinkle with the chives or scallions. Bake for 25–30 minutes, or until the quiche is puffy and lightly browned on top. Serve hot.

PÂTE BRISÉE

1   CUP ALL-PURPOSE FLOUR
2   PINCHES OF SALT
4   TABLESPOONS UNSALTED BUTTER,
    CUT IN PIECES
1   EGG
    A FEW DROPS OF ICE WATER (IF DOUGH IS
    TOO DRY)

In a mixing bowl, blend together the flour and salt. Cut in the butter and continue to blend. Add the egg yolk and incorporate into the dough. Add ice water if needed. Form into a ball and cover with plastic wrap. Chill for 2 hours before rolling out to a thickness of ¼ inch. When rolling out the dough, use either a floured surface or place it between two sheets of wax paper. Dough should be about 2 inches larger than the tart pan. Proceed according to recipe.

OIGNONS FARCIS / STUFFED ONIONS
ADAPTED FROM AUDOT'S
La cuisinière de la campagne et de la ville, 1857.

Serves 4

4   LARGE ONIONS
4   TABLESPOONS UNSALTED BUTTER
¼   POUND SAUSAGE MEAT
1   CUP FRESH WHITE BREAD CRUMBS, SOAKED
    IN MILK AND SQUEEZED DRY
    SALT
    FRESHLY GROUND BLACK PEPPER
    FRESHLY GRATED NUTMEG
1   TABLESPOON FINES HERBES (SEE NOTE ON
    PAGE 40)
1 ½ CUPS CHICKEN STOCK OR BROTH, HEATED

Preheat the oven to 350°F.

Peel the onions and scoop out and mince the centers. Put the onion shells into a buttered baking dish. In a skillet, heat half of the butter and add the minced onion centers, sausage meat, and bread crumbs. Season with salt, pepper, and nutmeg. Mix well and add the *fines herbes*. Cook over low heat for 10-15 minutes, stirring constantly.

Stuff the onion shells with the sausage mixture and dot them with the remaining butter. Pour stock around the onions and cover with aluminum foil. Bake for 30–40 minutes. When the onions are cooked, pour the pan juices into a small saucepan, set over high heat, and reduce by half. Pour over the onions and serve hot.

HARICOTS VERTS EN SALADE /
STRING BEAN SALAD

ADAPTED FROM DUBOIS'S *La cuisine classique*, 1867.

Serves 4

- 1 POUND UNBLEMISHED GREEN BEANS, ENDS SNIPPED
- ½ CUP SHALLOT VINAIGRETTE (RECIPE FOLLOWS)
  PINCH FRESHLY GROUND WHITE PEPPER
- ¼ CUP CHOPPED FRESH PARSLEY

In a large pot of salted boiling water, cook the string beans for 8–10 minutes, or until they are slightly tender when pricked with a fork. Drain them in a colander and allow to cool. Transfer the beans to a large bowl and pour the vinaigrette over them. Toss well, add pepper, and top with minced parsley. You can make the salad ahead of time and refrigerate before serving.

SHALLOT VINAIGRETTE

Makes ¼ cup

- 1 TABLESPOON RED WINE VINEGAR
- ½ TEASPOON SALT
- 3 TABLESPOONS OLIVE OR VEGETABLE OIL
- 1 SHALLOT, MINCED
- ½ TEASPOON DIJON MUSTARD

Combine all the ingredients in a small bowl and mix well with a small wire whisk. (You may also make the dressing in a cruet. Shake well before serving.)

POULET RÔTI AU ROMARIN /
ROSEMARY ROAST CHICKEN

ADAPTED FROM AUDOT'S
La cuisinière de la campagne et de la ville, 1857.

Serves 4–6

- 1 5-POUND ROASTING CHICKEN
- ½ LEMON
   SALT
   FRESHLY GROUND BLACK PEPPER
- 1 SMALL WHITE ONION, SLICED
- 3 TABLESPOONS UNSALTED BUTTER, SOFTENED
- 2 SPRIGS FRESH ROSEMARY

Preheat the oven to 350°F.

After rinsing and drying the chicken, rub the cavity with the cut lemon. Sprinkle with salt and pepper and place onion slices inside the chicken. Spread the softened butter on the outside of the chicken and sprinkle rosemary leaves on top. Season with salt and pepper.

Roast for about 1¼ hours, basting several times with the pan juices. The chicken is done if the juices run clear when a drumstick is pierced with a fork.

CLAFOUTI AUX CERISES / CHERRY FLAN
Adapted from Dubois's *La cuisine classique*, 1867.

Clafouti, or *clafoutis*—or spelled *clafoutian* when made with vegetables—is a summer harvest dish originating from the Limousin region in south central France. When fruit trees seem to bend under the weight of their yield, country folk whip together these simple, satisfying flanlike fruit desserts. While this dish is traditionally made with unstoned cherries, feel free to improvise with apricots, peaches, plums, or even raspberries or strawberries. The dish works best when fruit is already quite ripe.

Serves 4–6

3	CUPS VERY RIPE DARK CHERRIES, PITTED
½	CUP SUGAR
2	EGG YOLKS
1	EGG
½	CUP UNSALTED BUTTER, SOFTENED
1	CUP ALL-PURPOSE FLOUR
1 ½	TABLESPOONS KIRSCH
1	CUP MILK OR CREAM

Preheat the oven to 375°F.

When pitting the cherries, be careful not to break them. Place them in a bowl and set aside. To make the batter, combine the sugar and egg yolks, and when they are well blended, beat in the whole egg. Gradually add the butter and continue to beat. Add the flour and milk, alternating in thirds and continue stirring until the batter is very smooth. Add the kirsch and mix thoroughly.

Grease an 8- or 9-inch baking dish generously with butter and lay the cherries in the bottom. Pour the batter over the fruit and bake for 35–40 minutes on the lower rack of the oven. Serve warm.

[MENU № 7]

Au Restaurant de La Sirène

Potage à l'Oseille
SORREL SOUP

Artichauts à la Barigoule
ARTICHOKES WITH BACON AND HERBS

Coquilles Saint-Jacques
SCALLOPS IN BUTTER

Purée de Carottes aux Pommes de Terre
CARROT-POTATO PURÉE

Bifteck au Beurre d'Anchois
STEAK WITH ANCHOVY BUTTER

Mousse au Chocolat
CHOCOLATE MOUSSE

Sorbet à l'Abricot
APRICOT SORBET

Vins
WINES
Rully blanc (Chalonnais) / Chambertin Clos de Bèze

Café et Liqueurs
COFFEE AND LIQUEURS

THIS MENU PAYS HOMAGE to Vincent van Gogh, who painted *Le Restaurant de la Sirène* (1887) during one of his stays in Paris. Presented are the typical dishes one would find on the menus of the many hotel-restaurants that sprang up in the suburbs of the French capital during the last century. The featured soup, *Potage à l'Oseille*, was a popular nineteenth-century dish in France and is gaining popularity in the United States today. *Sorbet à l'Abricot* is a tribute to the Café Tortoni, whose sorbets were among the best to be found in the Paris of the mid-1800s.

POTAGE À L'OSEILLE / SORREL SOUP
ADAPTED FROM DUBOIS'S *La cuisine classique*, 1867.

Potage à l'Oseille, also known as *Potage Germiny*, was a very popular first-service dish during the nineteenth century, and frequently appeared on menus or in the indexes of cookbooks. During the last few years, it has become easier to obtain sorrel in the United States. Many farmers' markets and better grocery stores now carry it.

Serves 4–6

1	TABLESPOON UNSALTED BUTTER
¼	CUP FINELY CHOPPED SCALLIONS
½	POUND SORREL, FINELY CHOPPED
5	CUPS CHICKEN STOCK, HEATED
4	EGG YOLKS
2	CUPS LIGHT CREAM
	SALT
	FRESHLY GROUND BLACK PEPPER
	FRESHLY GRATED NUTMEG (OPTIONAL)

In a skillet, sauté the scallions in the butter until they are soft. Add the chopped sorrel and cook until wilted. Set aside.

In a large saucepan, bring the stock to a boil. Meanwhile, in a large bowl, beat together the egg yolks and cream. Add the stock a cup at a time to the egg and cream mixture, using a wire whisk to blend the ingredients. Return the mixture to the saucepan and cook until slightly thickened. Do not allow to boil.

Remove from the heat and stir in the sorrel and scallions. Add the salt, pepper, and nutmeg. Blend well and serve. If serving cold, refrigerate for several hours.

C. LAPLANTE

ARTICHAUTS À LA BARIGOULE /
ARTICHOKES WITH BACON AND HERBS

ADAPTED FROM DUBOIS's *La cuisine classique*, 1867.

Under the heading ARTICHAUT in the *Grand dictionnaire de cuisine,* Dumas gives a description of the artichoke and the plant on which it grows. He also provides his own version of *Artichauts à la Barigoule,* which more or less follows the classic recipe except for the addition of mushrooms.

Serves 4

- 12 SMALL ARTICHOKES
- 1 CUT LEMON
- ¼ CUP VEGETABLE OIL
- 2 OUNCES SMOKED HAM
- 1 SMALL ONION, MINCED
- 2 CLOVES GARLIC, CRUSHED
- 2 SPRIGS FRESH THYME
- 2 TABLESPOONS MINCED FRESH CHIVES
- ⅓ CUP DRY WHITE WINE
- ⅓ CUP WATER
  SALT
  FRESHLY GROUND WHITE PEPPER

Remove the tough outer leaves of the artichokes and cut off the tips of the remaining leaves. Spread open each artichoke so that the tough choke inside can be scooped out. Be sure to remove all of the choke. Rub with the cut lemon. Trim off the stems so that they are flush with the base of the artichokes.

Heat the oil in a deep casserole and add the ham. Cook for a minute or two, then add the onion and garlic. Sauté gently for a minute or two. Do not brown them. Add the artichokes, thyme, and chives and stir for a few minutes. Add the wine and water and season with salt and pepper. Cook, covered, over low heat for about 45 minutes, or until the artichokes are very soft. Serve warm on a serving dish.

COQUILLES SAINT-JACQUES /
SCALLOPS IN BUTTER

ADAPTED FROM DUBOIS's *La cuisine classique*, 1867.

Serves 4

- 24 SEA SCALLOPS
- 1 CUP MILK
- 2 TABLESPOONS UNSALTED BUTTER
- ½ LEMON
  SPRIGS OF FRESH TARRAGON (GARNISH)
- 1 LEMON, QUARTERED (GARNISH)

Preheat the oven to broiler setting.

Soak the scallops in a bowl of milk for about 10 minutes, then drain. Place them in a broiler pan lined with aluminum foil. Dot the scallops with butter and broil for about 5 minutes, or until done. Squeeze the juice of the half lemon over them. Garnish with the tarragon sprigs and lemon wedges and serve at once.

PURÉE DE CAROTTES AUX POMMES DE TERRE / CARROT-POTATO PURÉE

ADAPTED FROM AUDOT'S
La cuisinière de la campagne et de la ville, 1857.

Purées were a common dish in French cookery throughout the last century. A glance at the *Table des Mets* (list of dishes by course) in Audot's cookbook shows twelve different kinds of purées, including ones made from pumpkin, chicory, sorrel, turnips, lentils, onions, and mushrooms.

Serves 4–6

1	POUND CARROTS, PEELED
4	LARGE POTATOES, PEELED
3	TABLESPOONS UNSALTED BUTTER
½	CUP SOUR CREAM OR **CRÈME FRAÎCHE** (SEE PAGE 38)
	SALT
	FRESHLY GROUND WHITE PEPPER
	PINCH FRESHLY GRATED NUTMEG (OPTIONAL)

Cut carrots and potatoes into quarters and cook until tender in a large pot of boiling salted water. Drain well and return to the pot. Add the butter and mash. When the mixture is smooth, add the *crème fraîche* or sour cream and beat energetically until very smooth and creamy. Season with salt and pepper and, if desired, a little grated nutmeg. Serve hot.

BIFTECK AU BEURRE D'ANCHOIS / STEAK WITH ANCHOVY BUTTER

ADAPTED FROM DUBOIS'S *La cuisine classique*, 1867.

In his dictionary of food, Dumas describes the anchovy as a small sea fish no larger than a finger. He claims that this fish possesses naturally, as well as from the way it is customarily prepared, "a stimulating quality that facilitates digestion when it is used in moderation."

Serves 4

4	STEAKS, ½ POUND EACH
	OLIVE OIL
	SALT
	FRESHLY GROUND BLACK PEPPER
4	TABLESPOONS ANCHOVY BUTTER (RECIPE FOLLOWS)
	FRESH PARSLEY SPRIGS (GARNISH)

Brush each steak on both sides with the oil and broil under high heat to the desired degree of doneness. Season with salt and pepper. Spread each steak with a tablespoon of anchovy butter and transfer to a serving dish. Garnish with parsley.

ANCHOVY BUTTER

½	CUP UNSALTED BUTTER
3	LARGE ANCHOVY FILLETS, MASHED, OR 1 TABLESPOON ANCHOVY PASTE
3	DROPS LEMON JUICE
	FRESHLY GROUND WHITE PEPPER
	MINCED FRESH PARSLEY (OPTIONAL)

Cream the butter, then add the mashed anchovies a little at a time. Season to taste by adding the lemon juice, pepper, and, if desired, some minced parsley.

MOUSSE AU CHOCOLAT / CHOCOLATE MOUSSE

Adapted from Dubois's *La cuisine classique*, 1867.

Serves 8–10

- ½ POUND SEMISWEET CHOCOLATE
- 6 EGGS, SEPARATED
- 3 TABLESPOONS STRONG COFFEE OR WATER
- ¼ CUP GRAND MARNIER
- 2 CUPS HEAVY CREAM
- 6 TABLESPOONS SUGAR

Melt the chocolate in a double boiler or metal bowl over hot water. In a heavy-bottomed saucepan, combine the egg yolks and coffee and cook over very low heat, beating energetically with a wire whisk. When the yolks begin to thicken, add the Grand Marnier and continue beating. Cook until the mixture is thick and creamy. Remove from the heat.

Fold the melted chocolate into the egg mixture and transfer to a large mixing bowl. Whip the cream until it starts to thicken and add half of the sugar. Fold into the chocolate mixture. In a separate bowl, beat the egg whites and add the remaining sugar, continuing to beat until stiff. Fold into the chocolate mixture.

Spoon the mousse into a serving bowl or individual dessert dishes, soufflé dishes, or wineglasses. Chill before serving. Garnish with whipped cream if desired. (See recipe for *crème Chantilly* on page 65.)

SORBET À L'ABRICOT / APRICOT SORBET

Adapted from Dubois's *La cuisine classique*, 1867.

Sorbets and ice cream were all the rage in Paris during the Impressionist epoch. This recipe is a tribute to the Café Tortoni, where Parisian notables went to see and be seen, including Manet, who was quite the *flâneur*.

Serves 4–6

- 1 POUND WELL-RIPENED APRICOTS, HALVED AND PITTED
- ¾ CUP SUGAR
- 1 SCANT CUP WATER
- 1 TEASPOON VANILLA EXTRACT
  JUICE OF 1½ LEMONS
- 2 EGG WHITES, BEATEN STIFF
  FRESH MINT SPRIGS (GARNISH)

Purée the apricots in a blender or food processor. Make a syrup by combining the sugar, water, and vanilla in a small saucepan. Dissolve the sugar in the water and boil for 5 minutes. Add the apricot purée to the syrup. Allow to cool before folding in lemon juice and egg whites.

Pour the mixture into a shallow metal pan or ice cube trays and set in the freezer. When mixture is firm around the edges, remove from the freezer and beat well for about 1 minute. Return the mixture to the freezer for several hours or until it is firm. Serve the sorbet in coupe glasses and garnish each with a sprig of fresh mint.

[MENU № 8]

A Family Luncheon Chez Monet

Oeufs à la Coque
SOFT-BOILED EGGS

Gratin de Champignons
BAKED MUSHROOMS

Entrecôte Bordelaise
STEAK BORDELAISE

Pommes Frites
FRENCH-FRIED POTATOES

Salade Verte
GREEN SALAD

Compotes de Pêches
PEACH COMPOTE

Soufflé aux Marrons
CHESTNUT SOUFFLÉ

Vins
WINES
Saint-Romain (Côte de Beaune) / Château La Pelletrie (St.-Emilion)

Café et Liqueurs
COFFEE AND LIQUEURS

THIS MENU FEATURES SIMPLE, honest home cooking—the type most favored by Monet—and is organized around the dishes presented in the painting: *Oeufs à la Coque, Pommes Frites,* and *Salade Verte.* Included, too, are two dishes Monet especially loved: *Compote de Pêches* and *Soufflé aux Marrons.* A portrait of food and family, the work depicts Monet's young son Jean and his first wife, Camille. It captures the warmth of a lunch *en famille.*

OEUFS À LA COQUE / SOFT-BOILED EGGS
Adapted from Audot's
La cuisinière de la campagne et de la ville, 1857.

Under the heading Oeufs in his *Grand dictionnaire de cuisine,* Dumas wrote, "When an egg is fresh, we do not say that the only way to eat it is soft-boiled; but merely that this is the best way. Cooked thus, it loses none of its delicacy. The yolk is flavorful, the white milky; and if one has been sufficiently sybaritic to cook it in broth, and to see that it is neither over- nor under-cooked, one will eat a perfect egg."

Serves 4

4	EGGS, AT ROOM TEMPERATURE
	SALT
	FRESHLY GROUND BLACK PEPPER
	BAGUETTE OR PEASANT BREAD (OPTIONAL)

In a saucepan, boil enough water to cover the eggs. When the water reaches the boiling point, slide the eggs into pan using a wooden spoon. Cook for 3–4 minutes, or to the desired consistency. Serve in egg cups and season with salt and pepper. Serve with bread.

GRATIN DE CHAMPIGNONS / BAKED MUSHROOMS
Adapted from Claire Joyes's *Les carnets de cuisine de Monet*, 1989.

Monet was a great fan of mushrooms and liked to add morels, chanterelles, and wild mushrooms to his scrambled eggs. In his cooking journals, the painter includes fifteen recipes that call for mushrooms. Among these are Oxtail Stew from the Parisian restaurant Marguery, Veal Cutlets Milanese Style, Braised Pigeons, Chicken Chasseur, *Coq au Vin,* Cèpes Bordeaux Style, Mushroom Purée, and the Symbolist poet Stéphane Mallarmé's Recipe for Chanterelles (with bacon).

Serves 4

4	CUPS MUSHROOMS (MORELS, CÈPES, CHANTERELLES, OR CULTIVATED)
¼	CUP UNSALTED BUTTER
2	SHALLOTS, CHOPPED
1	CLOVE GARLIC, MINCED
1	TABLESPOON COGNAC
1	TABLESPOON DRIED UNSEASONED BREAD CRUMBS
2	TABLESPOONS HEAVY CREAM OR CRÈME FRAÎCHE (SEE PAGE 38)
½	TEASPOON SALT
	FRESHLY GROUND BLACK PEPPER

Preheat the oven to 450°F.

Wipe the mushrooms clean with a paper towel or kitchen towel. Do not submerge them in water. Slice into quarters. In a saucepan, melt the butter and add the shallots and garlic. Sauté until the onions are transparent but not brown. Add the mushrooms and cognac and cook for 2 minutes.

In a small bowl, combine the bread crumbs and cream and add to the mushrooms. Mix well and continue to cook for a few minutes more. Season with salt and pepper and transfer to a greased baking dish. Bake for 15 minutes or until the bread crumbs are lightly browned. Serve very hot.

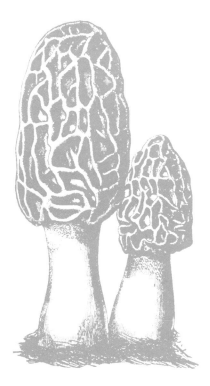

ENTRECÔTE BORDELAISE / STEAK BORDELAISE

ADAPTED FROM *Les 366 menus de Baron Brisse avec 1200 recettes et un calendrier nutritif*, 1875.

Serves 4

- 2 TABLESPOONS UNSALTED BUTTER
- 2 TABLESPOONS SHALLOTS, FINELY MINCED
- ⅔ CUP RED BORDEAUX WINE
- 1 ¼ CUPS BEEF BROTH
- 2 TEASPOONS LEMON JUICE
- 1 TABLESPOON CORNSTARCH
- 1 TABLESPOON FRESH PARSLEY, MINCED
- 4 STEAKS, ½ POUND EACH
  VEGETABLE OIL
  SALT
  FRESHLY GROUND BLACK PEPPER

In a small saucepan, melt the butter and sauté the shallots until they are soft. Add the wine, reserving two tablespoons, and reduce the liquid by half over high heat. Add the beef broth and lemon juice and simmer for fifteen minutes. Add the two tablespoons of wine to the cornstarch and mix well so there are no lumps. Add a little cold water if the mixture is too thick. Remove the saucepan from the heat and add the cornstarch mixture to the sauce a little at a time, stirring constantly. Return the saucepan to the stove and stir the sauce over medium heat until thickened. Add the parsley, mix thoroughly, and remove from the heat.

Brush the steaks on both sides with the vegetable oil. Season with salt and pepper and broil under high heat to the desired degree of doneness.

When the steaks are done, pour the pan juices into the wine sauce and stir. Correct the seasonings and serve with the steaks.

POMMES FRITES /
FRENCH-FRIED POTATOES
ADAPTED FROM DUBOIS'S *La cuisine classique*, 1867.

Serves 4–6
- 1 ½ POUNDS POTATOES (RUSSET OR IDAHO), PEELED
- 3 CUPS OIL FOR FRYING (APPROXIMATELY)
- SALT
- FRESHLY GROUND BLACK PEPPER

Cut the potatoes into rounds about ¼ inch thick. Rinse the potatoes in a bowl of cold water and dry them in a kitchen towel. Heat the oil in a deep skillet or flame-proof casserole until it is 375°F on a frying thermometer. (If you don't have a thermometer, test the oil by adding a potato slice. If it turns golden quickly, the oil is hot enough.)

Fry the potatoes until they are golden on both sides. As the potatoes are cooked, remove them with a slotted spoon to a plate lined with paper towels. Sprinkle with salt and pepper and transfer to a serving dish. Serve very hot.

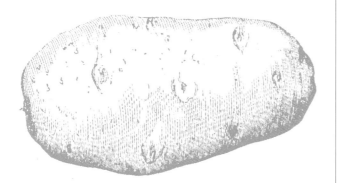

SALADE VERTE / GREEN SALAD
ADAPTED FROM JOYES'S *Les carnets de cuisine de Monet*, 1989.

Salads in the Monet household consisted of chicory with minced garlic and croutons, dandelion greens with cubes or strips of bacon, or lettuce from the kitchen garden (*potager*) with a simple oil and vinegar dressing, seasoned with coarse salt (*gros sel*) and an entire spoonful of ground black pepper! For this reason, there were always two bowls of salad on the table—one for Monet and his second wife, Alice Hoschedé (both pepper fiends); the other for everyone else.

Serves 4
- 2 SMALL FIRM HEADS BOSTON LETTUCE
- ⅓ CUP VINAIGRETTE SIMPLE (RECIPE FOLLOWS)
- FRESHLY GROUND BLACK PEPPER

Wash the lettuce and pat the leaves dry. Tear into bite-size pieces and place in a salad bowl. Pour the vinaigrette over the lettuce and toss. Season with black pepper.

VINAIGRETTE SIMPLE
Makes ¼ cup
- 1 TABLESPOON RED WINE VINEGAR
- ½ TEASPOON COARSE SALT
- 3 TABLESPOONS OLIVE OIL

Mix the ingredients in a small bowl and beat well with a small wire whisk. (You may also make the dressing in a cruet. Shake well before serving.)

COMPOTE DE PÊCHES / PEACH COMPOTE
ADAPTED FROM JOYES's *Les carnets de cuisine de Monet*, 1989.

Making fruit compotes is a healthy and delicious way to prepare fresh fruit. At Giverny, where the Monets grew their own fruits and vegetables, fruit compotes were frequently enjoyed. This recipe is an adaptation of one by Marguerite, Monet's family cook. She liked to serve her compotes in their own juice, with a cookie on the side. (See tea menu, page 99, for cookie recipes.)

Serves 4

- 1   CUP WATER (SUBSTITUTE ½ CUP WHITE WINE FOR ½ CUP WATER, IF DESIRED)
- ¾   CUP SUGAR
- 1   POUND PEACHES, WASHED, HALVED, AND PITTED
- 1   TEASPOON VANILLA

Make a syrup by boiling the water, sugar, and vanilla in a covered saucepan for 5–10 minutes. Add the peaches to the syrup two at a time and poach over medium heat for about eight minutes. Remove fruit with a slotted spoon and place in a bowl to cool. When the peaches are cool enough to handle, peel them. Place them in a bowl and pour the syrup over the fruit. Serve warm or chilled, garnished with whipped cream or vanilla ice cream if desired. (See recipe for *crème Chantilly* on page 65.)

SOUFFLÉ AUX MARRONS / CHESTNUT SOUFFLÉ
ADAPTED FROM JOYES's *Les carnets de cuisine de Monet*, 1989.

Under the heading for CHATAIGNE, Dumas writes in his *Grand dictionnaire de cuisine* that a chestnut is the fruit of a chestnut tree, a tree belonging to the beech family. He states that these nuts go very well with a variety of meats and can be used as a garnish for grilled meat. Monet was quite fond of chestnuts and included several dessert recipes calling for them. This is the most unusual one.

Serves 6

- 1   POUND CHESTNUTS
- 2   CUPS MILK
- 1   SMALL VANILLA BEAN, SPLIT LENGTHWISE, OR 2 TEASPOONS EXTRACT
- ¾   CUP SUGAR
- 1 ½ TABLESPOONS GRAND MARNIER
- 3   EGGS, SEPARATED

Shell the chestnuts in the following manner: With a small sharp knife, cut off a small piece of shell on each chestnut. Set the chestnuts in a pan of cold water. Bring to a boil and cook for about 60 seconds. With a slotted spoon, remove the chestnuts and peel off the shell and the dark inner skin. (If some of the chestnuts do not readily shed their skins, drop them back into the boiling water for another minute.)

Place the chestnuts, milk, vanilla bean, and sugar in a saucepan. Simmer, uncovered, over gentle heat for about ½ hour, or until the chestnuts have softened. Remove the chestnuts with a slotted spoon, draining them well, and place in a bowl. Discard the vanilla bean and reserve the cooking liquid.

Preheat the oven to 350°F.

Place the chestnuts in the bowl of a food processor and grind. Add a little of the cooking liquid if the mixture is too dry. Transfer the ground chestnuts to a mixing bowl, add the cooking liquid and Grand Marnier, and blend well. Add the egg yolks one at a time and beat until smooth.

Beat the egg whites into stiff peaks and fold them into the chestnut mixture. Grease a 6-cup soufflé dish and pour in the mixture. Bake for 30–40 minutes, or until the soufflé is well risen and golden on top.

[MENU Nº 9]

Tea for Two

Petits Sandwiches Assortis
ASSORTED TEA SANDWICHES

Palets au Miel
HONEY COOKIES

Madeleines
MADELEINES

Galettes aux Marrons
CHESTNUT COOKIES

Scones
SCONES

Pain de Gênes
ALMOND CAKE

Thé Noire de Chine
CHINESE BLACK TEA

Vins
WINES
Clos des Princes (Barsac) / Champagne Veuve Cliquot Rosé

CASSATT'S PORTRAIT OF TWO WOMEN (her sister, Lydia, and a guest) drinking tea and the elegant silver service are the inspiration behind this menu. During the nineteenth century, the French bourgeoisie eagerly adopted the custom of drinking tea from their British counterparts across the Channel. They called their late-afternoon collation "le five o'clock," even though it was served between four and six. The featured dishes—*Petits Sandwiches Assortis, Palets au Miel*, and *Madeleines*—are the traditional light fare that accompanied "le five o'clock." The velvety smoothness of the Clos des Princes and the quiet elegance of the Veuve Cliquot add an exciting touch to tea taking.

PETITS SANDWICHES ASSORTIS / ASSORTED TEA SANDWICHES
ADAPTED FROM AUDOT'S
La cuisinière de la campagne et de la ville, 1851.

Tea was considered a light, informal meal (*petit repas*)—one "*sans cérémonie.*" The tea itself was taken with a drop of cream and accompanied by sweet breads, pastries, *tartines* (buttered bread) with or without jelly or jam, and dainty little sandwiches of roast beef, ham, and cheese—served on *pain de mie* (white sandwich bread), not the traditional baguette.

Serves 2–4

	UNSALTED BUTTER, SOFTENED, AND/OR DIJON MUSTARD
8	SLICES WHITE BREAD, CRUSTS TRIMMED
2	THIN SLICES BOILED OR SMOKED HAM
4	THIN SLICES HARD SAUSAGE
2	THIN SLICES ROAST BEEF
2	THIN SLICES GRUYÈRE, EMMENTHAL, OR OTHER SWISS-TYPE CHEESE

Spread butter or mustard on the bread slices according to your preference. Make delicate sandwiches with the meats and cheese. (Use only 2 or 3 slices for each sandwich; do not overstuff.) Slicing diagonally, cut each sandwich into quarters or halves.

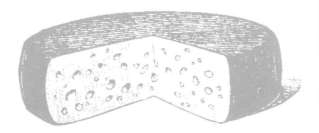

PALETS AU MIEL / HONEY COOKIES
ADAPTED FROM JOYES'S *Les carnets de cuisine de Monet*, 1989.

Makes 2 dozen

2	EGGS, BEATEN
1	CUP SIFTED CONFECTIONERS' SUGAR
¼	CUP CLOVER OR WILDFLOWER HONEY
1 ¼	CUPS SIFTED ALL-PURPOSE FLOUR
⅓	CUP FINELY CHOPPED WALNUTS

Preheat the oven to 325°F.

Combine the eggs and sugar in a mixing bowl and beat well, until mixture is smooth and creamy. Add the honey, continuing to mix, and then beat in the flour a little at a time. Add the nuts. Allow the mixture to rest for ½ hour.

Grease a baking sheet. Using 2 teaspoons, drop small mounds of cookie batter onto the baking sheet. Bake for 15 minutes, or until the cookies are a rich golden brown.

MADELEINES / MADELEINES

ADAPTED FROM JOYES's *Les carnets de cuisine de Monet*, 1989.

It was not only in Marcel Proust's household that madeleines were savored. Marguerite, the cook, would often bake these delicate little cakes for Monet and his family.

Makes 2 dozen

- ½ CUP UNSALTED BUTTER, SOFTENED
- 1 CUP GRANULATED SUGAR
- 4 EGGS, SEPARATED
- 1 TEASPOON VANILLA EXTRACT
     ZEST OF 1 LEMON
- 1 CUP SIFTED ALL-PURPOSE FLOUR
     CONFECTIONERS' SUGAR (OPTIONAL)

Preheat the oven to 400°F.

Generously grease the Madeleine molds. In a small bowl, cream together the butter and sugar, and add the egg yolks one at a time, beating well until the mixture is smooth. Add the vanilla, lemon zest, and flour, and mix well. In a large bowl, beat the egg whites until they form soft peaks. Fold the egg whites into the batter, a little at a time, until fully blended.

Fill each mold two-thirds full and bake until the cakes have risen and are moderately browned (about 12–14 minutes). Remove from pans to a wire rack and allow to cool. Dust lightly with confectioners' sugar.

GALETTES AUX MARRONS / CHESTNUT COOKIES

ADAPTED FROM JOYES's *Les carnets de cuisine de Monet*, 1989.

Chestnuts are a sure sign of late fall and the coming of winter. When these nuts have fallen from great spreading trees and have been eagerly harvested, they are roasted or puréed and added to a number of dishes. In the nineteenth century as well as today in France, chestnuts are eaten both *salé* in stuffings or ragouts and *sucré* in cookies or as fillings for cakes. Monet is said to have been a great fan of chestnuts, and he loved these cookies at tea time.

Makes 1½ dozen

- ½ CUP UNSALTED BUTTER
- 1 CUP UNSWEETENED CHESTNUT PURÉE
- ¾ CUP LIGHT BROWN SUGAR
- 3 EGGS, SEPARATED
- 1 TEASPOON VANILLA EXTRACT
- ¼ CUP CHOPPED TOASTED HAZELNUTS
     (OPTIONAL)

Preheat the oven to 350°F.

Grease muffin tins. Fill any empty molds with water when baking. In a medium-size saucepan, melt the butter over low heat, then add chestnut purée, sugar, egg yolks, and vanilla, stirring constantly. Heat through but do not boil. Remove from the heat.

In a mixing bowl, beat the egg whites until they form stiff peaks, then fold them into the cooled chestnut mixture with a spatula. Pour the batter into individual molds, top with hazelnuts if desired, and bake for 20 minutes, or until the *galettes* are firm.

SCONES / SCONES
ADAPTED FROM JOYES'S *Les carnets de cuisine de Monet*, 1989.

Scones were not a regular feature of high teas in France during the Impressionist epoch. It was probably during Monet's stay in England at the time of the Franco-Prussian War (1870–71) that the painter acquired a taste for these little semisweet cakes. An adventurous eater, Monet collected recipes wherever he went, whether to Paris for dinner *chez* Drouant or on trips abroad.

Makes about 1½ dozen

2	CUPS SIFTED ALL-PURPOSE FLOUR
2	TABLESPOONS SUGAR
3	TEASPOONS BAKING POWDER
½	TEASPOON SALT
5	TABLESPOONS UNSALTED BUTTER
1	EGG, BEATEN
¾	CUP HALF-AND-HALF

Preheat the oven to 425°F.

Sift the flour with the sugar, baking powder, and salt. Rub in the butter until it is in pea-size pieces, then add the beaten egg and about half of the half-and-half, stirring well until all of the flour is incorporated. Add the rest of the half-and-half and work the dough until it is soft, adding more liquid if necessary.

On a floured surface, turn out the dough and knead gently a dozen times. Roll out the dough to a thickness of ½ inch. Cut out circles with a glass and place on a well-greased baking sheet.

Bake for about 15 minutes, or until the scones have risen well and are golden brown on top. Serve hot with butter and/or your favorite jelly or jam.

PAIN DE GÊNES / ALMOND CAKE

ADAPTED FROM JOYES'S *Les carnets de cuisine de Monet*, 1989.

In the Monet household, tea was served each afternoon and usually consisted of a pot of Darjeeling, along with scones, and some type of cookie or cake made by Marguerite, the cook. In fine weather, tea was taken outdoors by the lily pond, under the lime trees, or on the balcony overlooking the painter's splendid gardens.

- ½ CUP UNSALTED BUTTER, SOFTENED
- 2 CUPS SIFTED CONFECTIONERS' SUGAR
- 5 EGGS, BEATEN
- ZEST OF 1 ORANGE
- 2⅓ CUPS GROUND ALMONDS
- 2 TABLESPOONS KIRSCH (OPTIONAL)
- ⅔ CUP SIFTED ALL-PURPOSE FLOUR
- ¾ CUP SLICED ALMONDS (OPTIONAL)

Preheat the oven to 350°F.

In a large mixing bowl, cream the butter and 1½ cups of the sugar until the mixture is smooth and light. Continue beating and add the eggs one at a time, mixing well after each addition. Beat in the ground almonds and orange zest and then add the kirsch. Grease an 8-inch cake pan. Pour the batter into the pan and bake for 40–45 minutes, or until the top of the cake is golden. Sprinkle with the remaining ½ cup of confectioners' sugar and top with the sliced almonds.

THÉ NOIRE DE CHINE / CHINESE BLACK TEA

"Le five o'clock" might be enjoyed at home or taken at any one of the many *salons de thé* that had opened along Paris's boulevards. Two popular spots were the Elysée-Palace on the Champs-Elysées and the Marquise de Sevignée on the Boulevard de la Madeleine.

[MENU № 10]

A Luncheon in the Garden

Potage de Carottes
CREAM OF CARROT SOUP

Epinards Etuvés au Beurre
SPINACH BRAISED IN BUTTER

Poulet à la Marengo
CHICKEN MARENGO

Riz à l'Indienne
INDIAN RICE

Blanquette de Veau
VEAL STEW

Crème au Caramel
CARAMEL CUSTARD

Sablés
SUGAR COOKIES

Fruits de Saison
FRESH PEACHES AND YELLOW PLUMS

Vins
WINES
Château Latour Leognan-Pessa (Graves) / Chiroubles (Beaujolais Cru)

Café et Liqueurs
COFFEE AND LIQUEURS

MONET'S HOME AT ARGENTEUIL, where the artist lived from 1871 to 1878, is the inspiration behind this menu. This luncheon menu features classic "cuisine bourgeoise"—*Potage de Carottes, Blanquette de Veau,* and *Crème Caramel,* along with an unusual preparation for rice. Although rice dishes were popular in nineteenth-century French cuisine, *Riz a l'Indienne* was still somewhat exotic. Its very name, a borrowing from another culture, reflects the century's colonial experiences.

POTAGE DE CAROTTES / CREAM OF CARROT SOUP

ADAPTED FROM AUDOT'S
La cuisinière de la campagne et de la ville, 1857.

Due to their versatility, carrots were an extremely popular vegetable in nineteenth-century French kitchens and were used in soups, purées, stews, casseroles, and salads. Dumas claimed that carrots purified the blood, and that if eaten in moderation, were not "unhealthful." He believed, too, that carrots contained oil and essential salts, and were therefore suitable to individuals of all ages and dispositions.

Serves 4

- 1   LEEK, THINLY SLICED (USE WHITE PART ONLY)
- 8   MEDIUM-SIZE CARROTS
- 5   CUPS VEGETABLE OR CHICKEN STOCK
- ¼   CUP UNSALTED BUTTER
- ½   CUP HEAVY CREAM OR HALF-AND-HALF
-     SALT
-     FRESHLY GROUND WHITE PEPPER
-     SPRIG OF FRESH DILL (GARNISH)

Sauté leek until transparent in a frying pan with 1 tablespoon of butter. Set aside. Wash the carrots but do not peel them; cut each carrot into quarters. Bring the stock to a boil in a large saucepan, add the carrots, and cook until soft. Remove the carrots and leek from the stock and purée in a blender or food processor. Return the purée to the stock and add the butter and heavy cream. Mix well and heat thoroughly (only if serving hot) over gentle heat. Season with salt and pepper. Garnish with a bit of dill. Serve hot or chilled.

EPINARDS ETUVÉS AU BEURRE / SPINACH BRAISED IN BUTTER

ADAPTED FROM THE
Nouveau manuel de la cuisine bourgeoise et économique, 1866.

In his formidable dictionary of food, Dumas wrote that lots of jokes were made about spinach because it was commonly believed that this leafy vegetable had no nutritional properties. "This is wrong," he stated. "Spinach, on the contrary, is nutritious and pleasing to the stomach, for which it is not the broom, if I may use such an expression, except in the sense that it so suits this organ that it is digested with remarkable ease."

Serves 4

- 2   POUNDS FRESH SPINACH, TOUGH STEMS REMOVED
- 3   TABLESPOONS UNSALTED BUTTER
-     SALT
-     FRESHLY GRATED WHITE PEPPER
-     FRESHLY GRATED NUTMEG
- 3   DROPS LEMON JUICE (OPTIONAL)

Wash the spinach in several changes of water to remove all of the sand. In a large pot, cook the spinach with the water that clings to the leaves plus an additional ¼–½ cup of water. The spinach will wilt rapidly. As soon as the spinach has wilted, remove it from the pot, squeeze out any remaining water, and chop finely. In a skillet, melt the butter and add the spinach, heating thoroughly. Season with salt, pepper, and nutmeg. Squeeze a few drops of lemon juice over the spinach if desired. Serve hot.

POULET À LA MARENGO / CHICKEN MARENGO
ADAPTED FROM THE
Nouveau manuel de la cuisine bourgeoise et économique, 1866.

Poulet à la Marengo and its offshoot recipe *Veau à la Marengo* enjoyed enormous popularity during the last century in France. The dish was created to celebrate Napoleon Bonaparte's victory over the Austrians in a battle that took place on June 14, 1800, near the village of Marengo, not far from Genoa, Italy.

Serves 4–6

4	TABLESPOONS VEGETABLE OIL
1	CLOVE GARLIC, MINCED
2	POUNDS BONELESS CHICKEN BREASTS, CUT INTO 2-INCH PIECES
2	SHALLOTS, MINCED
¼	POUND MUSHROOMS, SLICED THIN
4	TOMATOES, PEELED, SEEDED, AND CHOPPED
	SALT
¼	TEASPOON CAYENNE PEPPER
1	CUP DRY WHITE WINE
1	BOUQUET GARNI (SEE INSTRUCTIONS BELOW)
10	PEARL ONIONS
1	CUP SMALL GREEN OLIVES, PITTED
½	POUND PEELED RAW SHRIMP

Heat 2 tablespoons of the oil in a heavy-bottomed casserole over low heat and add the garlic and chicken. Sauté until chicken is lightly browned. Remove chicken to a plate and keep warm. Add the remaining oil and sauté the shallots, mushrooms, and tomatoes. Season with salt and cayenne pepper. Return the chicken to the pan and add the wine, *bouquet garni,* and pearl onions. Simmer, covered, over low heat for about 1 hour. Add the olives about 15 minutes before the cooking is finished. Add the shrimp 5 minutes before the cooking is finished. Do not overcook the shrimp. Remove the *bouquet garni* before serving. Serve very hot.

For the bouquet garni:
A *bouquet garni* consists of sprigs of fresh herbs tied together and wrapped in cheesecloth. For this recipe, use sprigs of parsley, thyme, and bay leaves. Tie the "bundle" well so that it doesn't come undone during cooking.

RIZ À L'INDIENNE / INDIAN RICE
ADAPTED FROM DUBOIS'S *La cuisine classique, 1867.*

From the beginning of the nineteenth century onward, rice became an important part of the French diet, particularly at formal meals in the first half of the century. The 1867 edition of *Les 366 menus de Baron Brisse* featured rice in sixty-seven menus, making it even more popular than the potato. Rice was eaten both *salé* (savory) and *sucré* (sweet). It was used either as an ingredient in a variety of kinds of soups, as an accompaniment to a main course, or as a dessert item in, for example, a *gâteau de riz* (rice tart) or *riz à l'impératrice* (a gourmet version of rice pudding). *Riz à l'Indienne* is fun to prepare and gives the rice a dry texture, although the grains remain fluffy.

Serves 4

6	CUPS WATER
	SALT
1	CUP LONG-GRAIN WHITE RICE

Preheat the oven to 350°F.

Bring salted water to a boil in a large saucepan. Add the rice and cook for 15 minutes, stirring occasionally. Drain the rice in a colander and rinse well with lukewarm water. Drain the rice again, place it in a clean kitchen towel, and wrap it so that it is entirely covered. (Be sure that the towel is not perfumed from laundry detergent or fabric softener because any fragrance will flavor the rice.) Put the "bundle" into a casserole dish and bake for 15–20 minutes, or until the grains separate when fluffed with a fork.

BLANQUETTE DE VEAU / VEAL STEW
ADAPTED FROM AUDOT'S
La cuisinière de la campagne et de la ville, 1857.

Veal was quite popular in France during the last century and nearly every part was served. Audot's cookbook contains an astounding sixty entries under the heading ENTRÉES DE VEAU, including recipes for veal scallops, cutlets, shoulder, stew, liver, kidneys, heart, brains, tail, ears, tongue, and feet.

Serves 6

2	TABLESPOONS VEGETABLE OIL
6	TABLESPOONS UNSALTED BUTTER
2½	POUNDS BONELESS BREAST OF VEAL, CUT INTO 2-INCH PIECES
2	CARROTS, DICED
2	ONIONS, DICED
2	LEEKS, THINLY SLICED (WHITE PART ONLY)
2	CLOVES GARLIC, MINCED
1	**BOUQUET GARNI** (SEE PAGE 110)
	SALT
	FRESHLY GROUND WHITE PEPPER
1	CUP THINLY SLICED MUSHROOMS
3	TABLESPOONS FLOUR
1	TABLESPOON MINCED FRESH TARRAGON
3	EGG YOLKS
1	CUP **CRÈME FRAÎCHE** (SEE PAGE 38)
	JUICE OF 1 LEMON

Heat 1 tablespoon of the oil and 3 tablespoons of the butter in a large sauté pan over high heat. Add the veal and sauté quickly on all sides without browning. Remove the meat from the pan with a slotted spoon and set aside. Add 1 tablespoon each of the oil and butter and sauté the carrots, onions, leeks, and garlic. Cook until the vegetables are soft, stirring frequently.

Return the meat to the pan and add the *bouquet garni.* Add just enough boiling water to barely cover the meat and season with salt and pepper. Bring to a boil, reduce the heat, and cover. Simmer for 1–1¼ hours, or until the veal is tender.

While the stew is cooking, quickly sauté the mushrooms in 1 tablespoon of the butter. Transfer meat, vegetables, and mushrooms to another pan and keep warm. Strain the cooking liquid through a fine sieve. Set the veal stock aside and skim the fat from the surface.

Heat the remaining tablespoon of butter in a saucepan and stir in the flour, cooking until it is almost golden. Add the strained veal stock, stirring constantly until the sauce is smooth and slightly thickened. Add the tarragon and simmer over low heat for 15 minutes. Beat together the egg yolks, *crème fraîche,* and lemon juice. Remove the sauce from the heat and beat in the egg yolk mixture.

Return the sauce to low heat and simmer gently until it thickens slightly. Be careful that the mixture does not boil. Add to the veal and vegetables, and heat. Test for seasoning and transfer to a warm serving dish.

CRÈME AU CARAMEL / CARAMEL CUSTARD

ADAPTED FROM DUBOIS'S *La cuisine classique*, 1867.

Serves 4–6

1½	CUPS SUGAR
¼	CUP WATER
3¾	CUPS MILK
1	VANILLA BEAN, SPLIT LENGTHWISE,
	OR 2 TEASPOONS VANILLA EXTRACT
4	WHOLE EGGS
6	EGG YOLKS

Preheat the oven to 325°F.

In a heavy-bottomed small saucepan, boil 1 cup of the sugar and the water until the syrup is slightly browned. Pour a little syrup at a time into an 8-cup mold to coat the bottom and sides. Dip the mold in cold water to stop the caramel from running.

In a saucepan, combine the milk and vanilla bean and bring to a boil. Remove the vanilla bean and keep the milk hot.

In a large bowl, beat together the eggs, egg yolks, and remaining ¾ cup sugar until very light. Gradually add the hot milk and stir until all the ingredients are well mixed. Pour the mixture into the mold and set in a baking pan of simmering water. Bake for 45–50 minutes. The custard is done when a knife inserted in the center comes out clean. Cool and unmold before serving.

SABLÉS / SUGAR COOKIES

ADAPTED FROM CARÊME'S *Le parfait Cordon Bleu*, C. 1870.

Makes 3 dozen

2	CUPS SIFTED ALL-PURPOSE FLOUR
¾	CUP UNSALTED BUTTER, SOFTENED
½	CUP GRANULATED SUGAR
¼	CUP CONFECTIONERS' SUGAR
6	EGG YOLKS, BEATEN
½	TEASPOON VANILLA EXTRACT (OPTIONAL)
½	TEASPOON SALT
½	TEASPOON GROUND CINNAMON
	CONFECTIONERS' SUGAR OR CINNAMON FOR
	DUSTING (OPTIONAL)

Preheat the oven to 350°F.

In a large mixing bowl, combine the flour, butter, and sugars. Mix well and add egg yolks, vanilla, salt, and cinnamon. Continue mixing until all of the flour has been incorporated. When the dough is smooth, form into a ball and refrigerate for 30 minutes. Roll out the dough between 2 sheets of wax paper to a ¼-inch thickness and cut with cookie cutters into the desired shapes. Grease a baking sheet and bake the cookies for 8–10 minutes or until lightly golden along the edges. Transfer the cookies to a wire rack and allow them to cool completely. Dust with confectioners' sugar or cinnamon if desired. (To achieve a fine, light dusting, place a teaspoon of confectioners' sugar or cinnamon in a flour sifter and sift over the cookies.)

[MENU № 11]

A Picnic at Chatou

Potage au Cresson
WATERCRESS SOUP

Quiche Lorraine
HAM AND CHEESE QUICHE

Chou-Fleur en Salade
CAULIFLOWER SALAD

Turbot aux Câpres
TURBOT WITH CAPERS

Lapin Sauté
SAUTÉED RABBIT

Charlotte aux Pommes
APPLE CHARLOTTE

Fruits de Saison
FRESH FRUIT: GRAPES AND APRICOTS

Vins
WINES
Riesling / Gevrey-Chambertin (Côte de Nuits)

IN HOMAGE TO GUY DE MAUPASSANT, who wrote of picnic parties, rowing expeditions, and some of the haunts of the Impressionist painters, this menu features *Lapin Sauté*, which was described in one of his short stories in the *Maison Tellier* collection. *Charlotte aux Pommes*, a nineteenth-century classic featured in many French cookbooks of the period, is a simple, delicious dessert.

POTAGE AU CRESSON / WATERCRESS SOUP
ADAPTED FROM DUBOIS's *La cuisine classique*, 1867.

Soup was an indispensable component of the first service of a formal meal during the last century in France. Under the heading POTAGE in the index of Gouffé's *Le livre de cuisine*, 146 recipes are listed. One of the chief reasons for this superabundance is that for a number of the soups, Gouffé gives directions for both *gras* (with meat) and *maigre* (without meat) preparations.

Serves 4

1   SMALL YELLOW ONION, CHOPPED
2   TABLESPOONS UNSALTED BUTTER
5   CUPS LOOSELY PACKED FRESH
    WATERCRESS, WASHED AND DRIED
    (USE ONLY LEAVES AND TENDER STEMS)
    PINCH OF SALT
    BLACK PEPPER, FINELY GROUND
5   CUPS CHICKEN STOCK, BOILING
2   EGG YOLKS, BEATEN
½   CUP HALF-AND-HALF
    WATERCRESS SPRIGS (GARNISH)

In a large covered saucepan, sauté the onion in the butter for 5–10 minutes over very low heat. The onion should be soft but not browned. Add the watercress and salt and continue to cook until the greens have wilted. Add the boiling chicken stock and simmer for 5 minutes, then purée in a food processor.

In a large mixing bowl, blend the egg yolks and cream. Add the puréed mixture to the eggs and half-and-half, a cup at a time. Use a wire whisk to blend the ingredients. Pour the mixture into a saucepan and cook for 1–2 minutes, but do not allow the soup to simmer.

Season with salt and pepper. Garnish with watercress sprigs and serve hot or cold. If serving cold, refrigerate the soup, covered, for at least 4 hours before serving.

QUICHE LORRAINE / HAM AND CHEESE QUICHE
ADAPTED FROM DUBOIS's *La cuisine classique*, 1867.

Serves 4–6

1   CUP LIGHT CREAM OR HALF-AND-HALF
3   EGGS, BEATEN
1   RECIPE **PÂTE BRISÉE** (SEE PAGE 77)
2   OUNCES SMOKED HAM, CUT INTO SMALL
    PIECES
2   OUNCES GRUYÈRE, EMMENTHAL, OR OTHER
    SWISS-TYPE CHEESE, GRATED
    DASH OF FRESHLY GRATED NUTMEG
    (OPTIONAL)

Preheat the oven to 350°F.

In a bowl, mix the cream and eggs together. Beat until smooth.

Roll out the pastry, lay it in a 9-inch pie plate, and refrigerate for 20 minutes. When pastry has thoroughly chilled, remove from the refrigerator. Sprinkle the ham and the grated cheese on the bottom of the pastry shell and pour the egg mixture on top. Add grated nutmeg if desired. Place the quiche in the oven and bake for 30–35 minutes, or until the top is puffy and golden brown. Serve hot or at room temperature.

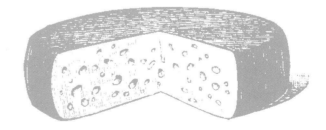

CHOU-FLEUR EN SALADE / CAULIFLOWER SALAD

ADAPTED FROM DUBOIS'S *La cuisine classique*, 1867.

Serves 6–8

1 HEAD UNBLEMISHED CAULIFLOWER
½ CUP FINES HERBES VINAIGRETTE
(SEE PAGE 40)

Wash the cauliflower and separate the flowerets from the base using a sharp knife. Plunge the flowerets into a pot of salted boiling water and cook for about 10 minutes, or until tender yet firm. Do not overcook. Drain well in a colander and transfer to a mixing bowl. Make the vinaigrette and pour over the cauliflower. Mix well and allow to "marinate" several hours before serving chilled or at room temperature.

TURBOT AUX CÂPRES / TURBOT WITH CAPERS

ADAPTED FROM THE
Nouveau manuel de la cuisine bourgeoise et économique, 1866.

In his *Grand dictionnaire de cuisine*, Dumas includes an entry for turbot and provides several recipes for its preparation. For *Kadgiori de Turbot*, or *Turbot Kedgeree*, he writes jokingly, "This dish, of Indian origin, is nowadays regularly served in England, which seems to have become a colony of India."

Serves 4

2 TEASPOONS ANCHOVY PASTE
2 TEASPOONS DIJON MUSTARD
½ CUP UNSALTED BUTTER
2 TABLESPOONS FRESHLY SQUEEZED LEMON JUICE
2 TABLESPOONS DRAINED CAPERS
4 FILLETS OF TURBOT (FLOUNDER OR SOLE MAY BE SUBSTITUTED)
   SALT
   FRESHLY GROUND BLACK PEPPER
1 TABLESPOON OLIVE OIL
1 TEASPOON CHOPPED CHIVES
   LEMON WEDGES (OPTIONAL)

In a small saucepan, combine the anchovy paste, mustard, and butter. Add the lemon juice and stir over low heat. Cook for a few minutes, until the mixture is creamy. Remove from the heat and add the capers.

Rinse the fillets and dry them. Sprinkle with salt and pepper. In a skillet, heat the oil, and when the pan is hot, lay in the fish and cook, covered, over medium heat for 8–10 minutes. Transfer the fish to a platter or individual plates and cover with the caper sauce. Sprinkle the chives over the fish and serve at once. Serve with the lemon wedges if desired.

LAPIN SAUTÉ / SAUTÉED RABBIT

ADAPTED FROM DUBOIS'S *La cuisine classique*, 1867.

This dish is a tribute to Renoir, who is known to have performed miracles with a rabbit in Monet's kitchen one afternoon. During the 1870s, when Monet was still very much the starving artist, Renoir, whose parents lived not far from Monet near Argenteuil, was frequently called upon to bail out not only the artist but also Monet's first wife, Camille Doncieux. At the start of his career, Monet was often penniless and unable to provide for his wife and son. One afternoon when there was nothing to eat *chez* Monet and a guest was expected for lunch to celebrate his receipt of a prestigious literary prize, Renoir came to the rescue. Bringing a rabbit from his parents' house, he managed to make three different dishes from it—a soup, a terrine, and a stew—with the guest never suspecting that the dishes had all come from a single source!

Serves 4–6

5   TABLESPOONS UNSALTED BUTTER
2   TABLESPOONS VEGETABLE OIL
1   RABBIT, ABOUT 3 POUNDS, CUT INTO PIECES
3   SPRIGS FRESH THYME
1   BAY LEAF, CRUMBLED
4   SHALLOTS, FINELY CHOPPED
½   POUND MUSHROOMS, THINLY SLICED
1   CUP DRY WHITE WINE
1   CUP CHICKEN STOCK
2   TABLESPOONS TOMATO PASTE
    SALT
    FRESHLY GROUND BLACK PEPPER
    FRESH THYME SPRIGS (GARNISH)

Preheat the oven to 325°F.

In a flameproof casserole, heat 2 tablespoons of the butter and the vegetable oil, and brown the rabbit pieces. Add 2 more tablespoons of butter, the thyme sprigs, and the bay leaf to the casserole. Season with salt and pepper. Cover and stew the rabbit in the oven for 45 minutes, stirring occasionally.

In a skillet, heat the remaining tablespoon of butter and cook the shallots and mushrooms until they are tender. Moisten with the white wine. Boil to reduce the wine by half. Add the chicken stock and tomato paste. Stir well to blend all the ingredients.

Return the liquid to a boil and reduce it a little. When the rabbit is cooked, add the mushroom mixture to the casserole and simmer on top of the stove for 5 minutes. Transfer the rabbit pieces to a shallow serving dish and garnish with sprigs of thyme.

CHARLOTTE AUX POMMES / APPLE CHARLOTTE

ADAPTED FROM *Les 366 menus de Baron Brisse avec 1200 recettes et un calendrier nutritif*, 1875.

In his *Grand dictionnaire de cuisine*, Dumas provides two recipes for charlottes—one for apricot charlotte and another for apple charlotte. The latter recipe is a jazzed-up version, calling for raspberry-flavored red currant jelly or apricot jam to be placed in the center of the stewed fruit.

Serves 6–8

- 10 MEDIUM-SIZE APPLES (DO NOT USE A TART VARIETY)
- ¾ CUP UNSALTED BUTTER
- ½ CUP LIGHT BROWN SUGAR
- ¼ TEASPOON GROUND CINNAMON
- 1 VANILLA BEAN, SPLIT LENGTHWISE, OR 2 TEASPOONS VANILLA EXTRACT
- 4 TABLESPOONS APRICOT PRESERVES, HEATED
- 12 SLICES WHITE BREAD, CRUSTS TRIMMED

Preheat the oven to 300°F.

Make a compote by peeling and coring the apples, then cutting them into small pieces. Put them in a saucepan with ¼ cup of the butter and cook over gentle heat until soft. Stir frequently to prevent sticking. Add the sugar, cinnamon, and vanilla bean or extract. Continue cooking for 15 minutes, or until the compote is thick. Remove the vanilla bean if using. Add the apricot preserves and blend well.

Melt the remaining butter in a skillet a little at a time, as needed, and quickly sauté the bread until golden on both sides. Line a 6–8-cup charlotte mold with 9 bread slices. Spoon the compote into the mold, and cover the top with the remaining 3 bread slices. Bake for 30–35 minutes. Let cool and then chill in the refrigerator before unmolding. Serve alone or with *crème Chantilly* (see recipe on page 65).

[MENU № 12]

Au Moulin de La Galette

Soupe à l'Oignon Gratinée
ONION SOUP GRATINÉE

Omelette au Lard
BACON OMELETTE

Salade de Pommes de Terre
POTATO SALAD

Croque Monsieur
GRILLED HAM AND CHEESE SANDWICH

Terrine de Foie Gras
TERRINE OF FOIE GRAS

Galettes
FLAT CAKES

Beignets de Pommes
APPLE FRITTERS

Vins
WINES
Juliénas (Beaujolais Cru) /Château Guiraud-Dauphin (Sauternes)

Café et Liqueurs
COFFEE AND LIQUEURS

THIS MENU IS INSPIRED by Renoir's joyous 1876 portrait of the Moulin de la Galette, an open-air dance hall near his studio in the Montmartre section of Paris. The establishment's name came from the *galettes*—flat cakes (sweet or savory)—traditionally served with drinks. Besides the *galettes,* the menu features the snack-like fare served in Parisian *guinguettes* (open-air dining or dancing establishments) of the last century and still popular today in modern-day cafés: *Omelette au Lard, Croque Monsieur,* and *Salade de Pommes de Terre.*

SOUPE À L'OIGNON GRATINÉE / ONION SOUP GRATINÉE

ADAPTED FROM GOUFFÉ's *Le livre de cuisine*, 1867.

Serves 4-6

- 5 TABLESPOONS UNSALTED BUTTER
- 6 MEDIUM-SIZE SWEET ONIONS, THINLY SLICED
- 6 CUPS BOILING STOCK (CHICKEN OR BEEF)
- 12 SLICES FRENCH BREAD
- 1 ½ CUPS GRATED GRUYÈRE, EMMENTHAL, OR OTHER SWISS-TYPE CHEESE
  SALT
  FRESHLY GROUND BLACK PEPPER

Preheat the oven to 400°F.

Melt half of the butter in a large skillet. Add the onions and cook until they are transparent. Add the stock and simmer over low heat for about 30 minutes. Toast the bread, spread with the remaining butter, and lay in the bottom of a casserole. Sprinkle the bread slices with the cheese and cover with the boiling stock and onions. Place the casserole, uncovered, in the oven for 10–15 minutes, or until the cheese on top begins to bubble. Season with salt and pepper and serve very hot.

OMELETTE AU LARD / BACON OMELETTE

ADAPTED FROM CARÊME's *Le parfait Cordon Bleu*, C. 1870.

Under the heading OMELETTE in the *Grand dictionnaire de cuisine*, Dumas provides recipes for a *fines herbes* omelette, a strawberry dessert omelette, and a dish he refers to as an Arab omelette, which calls for ostrich or flamingo eggs. To serve the *fines herbes* omelette, Dumas provides the following instructions: "Have a platter ready which has been buttered with the freshest possible butter and sprinkled with some more fresh *fines herbes*. Turn out the omelette on to this platter and serve it while it is still dribbling. Excuse the use of this last word, but each art has its own language, which must be employed to make oneself understood by the initiated."

Serves 2

- ¼ CUP DICED SMOKED BACON
- 4 TABLESPOONS UNSALTED BUTTER
- 6 EGGS
- 1 TABLESPOON WATER OR MILK
  SALT
  FRESHLY GROUND BLACK PEPPER

In a skillet, sauté the bacon in 2 tablespoons of the butter until it just begins to brown. Remove from the heat. In a mixing bowl, beat the eggs and add the water or milk. Add the bacon to the beaten eggs. Heat the remaining butter in the skillet or in an omelette pan, swirling the pan so that sides are also coated. Pour in the egg mixture and make an omelette in the usual way (see page 53 for instructions). Season with salt and pepper and serve immediately.

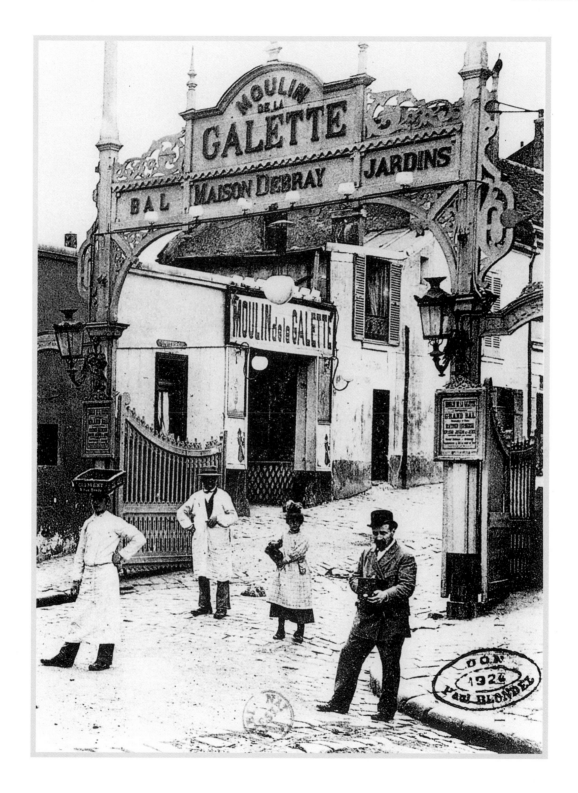

SALADE DE POMMES DE TERRE /
POTATO SALAD

ADAPTED FROM CARÈME's *Le parfait Cordon Bleu*, C. 1870.

Of the potato, Dumas writes in his dictionary of food, "This excellent vegetable was brought from Virginia by the English admiral Walter Raleigh in 1585, and has since then preserved people from famine." Dumas states that the potato provides real nourishment and is not only healthful but inexpensive. "Its preparation," he writes, "has this agreeable and advantageous aspect for the working class, that it involves practically no trouble or expense. The alacrity with which one observes children eating baked potatoes, and feeling all the better for them, proves that they suit all dispositions."

Serves 4–6

- 1 POUND NEW POTATOES, WASHED AND QUARTERED
- 1 DOUBLE RECIPE FOR DIJON MUSTARD VINAIGRETTE (RECIPE FOLLOWS)
  FRESHLY GROUND WHITE OR BLACK PEPPER
- 1 TABLESPOON CHOPPED CHIVES

Boil the potatoes in a pot of generously salted water until tender but firm when pricked with a fork. Drain in a colander. Transfer the potatoes to a serving bowl and add the vinaigrette. Mix well and season with pepper. Sprinkle chives over the potatoes and serve warm or chilled.

DIJON MUSTARD VINAIGRETTE

- 1 TABLESPOON RED WINE VINEGAR (OR VINEGAR OF CHOICE)
- ½ TEASPOON SALT
- 3 TABLESPOONS OLIVE OR VEGETABLE OIL
- 1 SHALLOT, MINCED
- 2 TEASPOONS DIJON MUSTARD

In a cruet, mix together all the ingredients and shake well. (Or mix in a small bowl and beat well with a whisk.)

CROQUE MONSIEUR /
GRILLED HAM AND CHEESE SANDWICH

ADAPTED FROM MME. C. DURANDEAU's *Guide de la bonne cuisine*, 1887.

Serves 4

- 3 TABLESPOONS UNSALTED BUTTER, SOFTENED
- 8 SLICES WHITE BREAD, CRUSTS TRIMMED
- 4 SLICES BOILED OR SMOKED HAM
- 4 SLICES GRUYÈRE, EMMENTHAL, OR OTHER SWISS-TYPE CHEESE
- ¼ CUP GRATED CHEESE (ONE OF THE ABOVE)

Preheat the broiler.

Butter the bread slices on one side. Trim the ham and cheese slices to fit on the bread without extending over the sides. Place the ham and cheese on 4 of the bread slices and top with the other 4 slices. Dot the outsides with butter. Place on a broiler rack and broil until golden. Turn over to broil other side and sprinkle with the grated cheese. When cheese is bubbly, remove and serve immediately.

TERRINE DE FOIE GRAS / TERRINE OF FOIE GRAS
ADAPTED FROM AUDOT'S
La cuisinière de la campagne et de la ville, 1857.

While this is a dish that very much captures the spirit of Paris's many eateries during the last century, it is, alas, rather complicated to make at home. This recipe has been modified for modern-day use. The process is not as grand or complicated as its nineteenth-century version, but the result is equally delicious.

½ POUND UNSALTED BUTTER, SOFTENED
3 SHALLOTS, MINCED
1 CLOVE GARLIC, MINCED
1 POUND CHICKEN LIVERS
1 TEASPOON SALT
¼ TEASPOON GROUND CLOVES
2 TEASPOONS DRY MUSTARD
½ TEASPOON DRIED THYME
½ TEASPOON FRESHLY GRATED NUTMEG
2 TABLESPOONS PORT
2 TABLESPOONS CHOPPED FRESH PARSLEY
¼ TEASPOON FRESHLY GROUND PEPPER

In a skillet, melt a third of the butter and sauté the shallots and garlic until soft. Add the chicken livers and cook until they lose their very red color, but do not overcook. They should still be light pink inside. Remove the livers, shallots, and garlic from the pan and purée them in a food processor.

Add the remaining butter and the salt, cloves, mustard, thyme, nutmeg, and port. Mix thoroughly. Add the parsley and pepper, and blend together. Pack the chicken liver mixture into a terrine or rectangular loaf pan. Chill thoroughly and serve with buttered bread or toast rounds.

GALETTES / FLAT CAKES
ADAPTED FROM JOYES'S *Les carnets de cuisine de Monet*, 1989.

Serves 6–8

2 CUPS SIFTED ALL-PURPOSE FLOUR
1 ½ TEASPOONS SALT
1 CUP UNSALTED BUTTER, SOFTENED
½ CUP LIGHT CREAM
1 EGG YOLK
CONFECTIONERS' SUGAR FOR DUSTING

Preheat the oven to 350°F.

In a large mixing bowl, combine the flour, salt, butter, and cream. Mix well and form a dough. Flour a clean cutting board or other work surface and roll out the dough into a square. Fold the dough over onto itself and cover with a damp cloth to rest for 15 minutes. Fold the dough again and let it rest under the damp cloth for another 15 minutes.

Roll the dough out into a large circle to a thickness of ¼ inch and place it on a well-greased baking sheet. With a knife, make a tic-tac-toe pattern on top of the dough and brush with the beaten egg. Bake until fully cooked and golden on top, about 45 minutes. Allow to cool completely. Dust with confectioners' sugar before serving.

BEIGNETS DE POMMES / APPLE FRITTERS

Adapted from *Les 366 menus de Baron Brisse*
avec 1200 recettes et un calendrier nutritif, 1875.

In nineteenth-century France, apples were used in a variety of ways, much as they are today. Cider, native to Normandy, was produced, as were jams, marmalades, and a number of desserts such as *Tarte aux Pommes, Tarte Tatin* (page 151), *Charlotte aux Pommes* (page 121), and of course *Beignets de Pommes.*

Serves 4–6

    6   MEDIUM-SIZE TART APPLES
    ½   CUP GRANULATED SUGAR
    ¼   TEASPOON GROUND CINNAMON
    ¼   TEASPOON FRESHLY GRATED NUTMEG
    ½   CUP RUM OR CALVADOS
    4   CUPS (APPROXIMATELY) VEGETABLE OIL
        CONFECTIONERS' SUGAR, SIFTED

For the batter:

    1 ¾   CUPS SIFTED ALL-PURPOSE FLOUR
    2   TABLESPOONS VEGETABLE OIL
    2   TABLESPOONS UNSALTED BUTTER, MELTED
    ¼   TEASPOON SALT
    2   EGGS
    ¼   CUP MILK

Wash, peel, core, and coarsely chop the apples. Put them in a small bowl; cover with the sugar, cinnamon, and nutmeg; and pour the rum or calvados over them. Mix well and let stand for 2–3 hours, stirring from time to time.

In another bowl, make the batter by combining the flour, oil, melted butter, salt, eggs, and milk. Beat until thoroughly mixed and quite smooth. Let the batter rest for 2–3 hours. Add the apple mixture to the batter.

Heat the oil for frying in a large saucepan or deep-fryer. Before cooking the *beignets*, the oil should be at 375°F (if you don't have a frying thermometer, test by frying 1 fritter). Make fritters by dropping the batter into the hot oil in generous tablespoonfuls. Fry until golden. Remove with a slotted spoon and drain well on paper towels. Sprinkle the *beignets* with confectioners' sugar and serve on a plate lined with a napkin to absorb any excess oil.

A Luncheon Chez Toulouse-Lautrec

Pois Chiches aux Epinards
SPINACH AND CHICKPEAS

Poireaux au Vin Rouge
LEEKS IN RED WINE

Poule Verte
GREEN "CHICKEN"

Homard à l'Américaine
LOBSTER AMERICAN STYLE

Salade de Pissenlits
SALAD OF DANDELION GREENS

Fromages Assortis
ASSORTED CHEESES: PORT SALUT, CAMEMBERT, CHÈVRE

Serpent du Couvent
THE CONVENT SERPENT

Vins
WINES
*Condrieu (Côtes du Rhône; white from Viognier grapes) /
Tavel (Rosé from lower Côtes du Rhône)*

Café et Liqueurs
COFFEE AND LIQUEURS

INSPIRED BY TOULOUSE-LAUTREC's passion for dining, entertaining, and his off-beat sense of humor, this menu presents several of his specialties. The lobster dish is a nineteenth-century classic often featured on restaurant menus and in cookbooks of the time. The other dishes are either Toulouse-Lautrec's interpretations of French classics, the *Poireaux au Vin Rouge*, for example, or they are his own inventions, inspired by the cuisines of other cultures or simply by his unusual imagination.

POIS CHICHES AUX EPINARDS /
SPINACH AND CHICKPEAS

Adapted from Henri de Toulouse-Lautrec and
Maurice Joyant's *L'art de la cuisine*, 1966.

Serves 6

2	CUPS DRIED CHICKPEAS
4	TABLESPOONS OLIVE OIL
2	CLOVES GARLIC, MINCED
3	TOMATOES, PEELED, SEEDED, AND CHOPPED
1/4	CUP FINELY CHOPPED PARSLEY
1/3	CUP SLIVERED ALMONDS
	SMALL HANDFUL HAZELNUTS
	PINCH OF GROUND SAFFRON
	PINCH OF GROUND CINNAMON
	PINCH EACH OF SALT, WHITE PEPPER, AND CAYENNE PEPPER
1	POUND SPINACH, WASHED, STEMS REMOVED, AND WILTED
1	HARD BOILED EGG, PEELED AND CHOPPED
1/2	POUND GARLIC SAUSAGE

Soak the chickpeas overnight in water to cover. Rinse well and place in a pot of salted water. Cook for 20–25 minutes, or until the beans are tender but not soft. Be careful not to overcook them. Drain, reserving 1½ cups of the liquid. Heat the oil in a skillet and sauté the garlic, tomatoes, and parsley until they just begin to brown.

In a large saucepan, combine the reserved liquid, tomato mixture, chickpeas, and nuts. Add the saffron, cinnamon, salt, white pepper, and cayenne. Cook over medium heat until the liquid has almost evaporated.

Chop the wilted spinach and add to the mixture. Add the chopped egg. Slice the sausage into thick rounds and quickly heat them in a skillet. Place the chickpea "casserole" on a serving platter and surround with the sausage rounds.

POIREAUX AU VIN ROUGE /
LEEKS IN RED WINE

Adapted from Toulouse-Lautrec and Joyant's
L'art de la cuisine, 1966.

These pretty pink leeks will no doubt be cause for some "oohing" and "ahhing" around the table—precisely the effect Lautrec hoped to achieve. For this dish, Lautrec specifically told the reader-cook not to add any scallions, garlic, or onions, but encouraged the use of cayenne pepper and/or cloves.

Serves 4–6

12	LEEKS, ENDS AND GREEN TOPS TRIMMED
1/2	POUND DICED BACON OR SMOKED HAM
1 1/2	CUPS DRY RED WINE
3/4	CUP WATER OR CHICKEN BROTH
	SALT
	FRESHLY GROUND WHITE PEPPER
3/4	TEASPOON GROUND CLOVES
1	EGG YOLK
2 1/2	TABLESPOONS DRIED BREAD CRUMBS
2	TEASPOONS CHOPPED FRESH PARSLEY

Wash the leeks, dry them, and cut in half lengthwise. Place the bacon or ham in a large sauté pan. Put the leeks on top and cover with the red wine and water. Season with salt, pepper, and ground cloves. Cook over low heat for about 1 hour. When the leeks are rosy and still firm, transfer to a baking dish.

Preheat the oven to 300°F.

In a small bowl, mix about ½ cup of the cooking liquid with the egg yolk. Pour the mixture over the leeks. Mix together the bread crumbs and parsley, and sprinkle on top of the leeks. Bake for 20–25 minutes, or until, as Lautrec directs, "the dish has thickened and the leeks don't swim about."

Dîner des Tarnais

POULE VERTE / GREEN "CHICKEN"
ADAPTED FROM TOULOUSE-LAUTREC AND JOYANT'S
L'art de la cuisine, 1966.

This is Toulouse-Lautrec's unusual version of a *galantine de volaille*—a boned chicken dish with aspic. In fact, it more closely resembles stuffed cabbage in its use of the kale leaves to wrap the meat filling. With any luck, and if your guests are sufficiently soused, this dish may resemble a green chicken after all.

Serves 4

1	HEAD KALE (ABOUT 1 POUND)
1/3	POUND GROUND PORK
1/3	POUND GROUND VEAL
1/3	POUND SAUSAGE MEAT
1/2	CUP FRESH BREAD CRUMBS
1/3	CUP CHOPPED FRESH PARSLEY
1/4	CUP CHOPPED SCALLIONS (WHITE PART ONLY)
2	EGGS, BEATEN
1/3	CUP MILK (USE MORE IF NEEDED)
	SALT
	FRESHLY GROUND WHITE PEPPER
1	QUART (APPROXIMATELY) CHICKEN STOCK OR WATER
3	NEW POTATOES, QUARTERED AND BOILED

Preheat the oven to 350°F.

In a large pot of salted boiling water, blanch the kale. Let drain in a colander. When it is cool enough to handle, take out the heart and chop it, reserving the large outer leaves to wrap the stuffing. In a bowl, mix together the ground meats, bread crumbs, parsley, scallions, salt, and pepper. Add the chopped kale, eggs, and milk, and blend.

Roll the stuffing up in individual kale leaves and tie each "green chick" with string (toothpicks may be used instead). Place in a casserole with enough chicken broth and/or water to cover and bake, covered, for 1–1¼ hours. With a slotted spoon, remove each "chick" carefully from the casserole and place on a large serving dish.

Serve in a mound, surrounded by the boiled quartered potatoes. Lautrec instructed that this dish be presented in such a way as "to give the appearance of a galantine of fowl."

HOMARD À L'AMÉRICAINE / LOBSTER AMERICAN STYLE
ADAPTED FROM TOULOUSE-LAUTREC AND JOYANT'S
L'art de la cuisine, 1966.

This is Toulouse-Lautrec's version of the well-loved nineteenth-century classic lobster dish. It is included here to commemorate the boiler-room supper hosted by the artist and Monsieur Joyant aboard a freight ship off the coast of Brittany.

Serves 2

2	LIVE LOBSTERS, 1 ½ POUNDS EACH
⅓	CUP OLIVE OIL
3	TABLESPOONS UNSALTED BUTTER
2	TABLESPOONS FINELY CHOPPED ONION
1	CLOVE GARLIC, MINCED
1	STALK CELERY, FINELY CHOPPED
1	SMALL CARROT, DICED
3	FIRM TOMATOES, PEELED, SEEDED, AND CRUSHED
3	TABLESPOONS CHOPPED FRESH PARSLEY
3	SPRIGS FRESH TARRAGON, CHOPPED
⅓	BOTTLE DRY WHITE WINE
	SALT TO TASTE
	PINCH OF CAYENNE PEPPER
¼	CUP BRANDY OR SHERRY

Split the lobsters in half lengthwise and cut the tails into 3 or 4 pieces. Crack the claws with a cleaver. Clean out the lobsters, discarding the stomach sacks and intestines but reserving the coral and liver for the sauce. In a large skillet, heat the oil. Add the lobster and cook, stirring, until the shells turn red. Transfer to a hot platter.

Melt the butter in the same skillet and add the onion, sautéing until transparent. Add the other vegetables, herbs, and wine and simmer for about 30 minutes. Return the lobster to the skillet. Season with salt and cayenne pepper and cook, covered, for 5 minutes.

Transfer the lobster to a serving dish and keep warm. Add brandy or whiskey to the sauce and cook over high heat until reduced by a third. In a small bowl or cup, mash the lobster coral and liver with a small amount of butter. Remove the sauce from the heat and mix in the coral butter. Pour the sauce over the lobster and serve hot. (The dish may be served on top of rice. See page 110 for *Riz à l'Indienne* / Indian Rice.)

SALADE DE PISSENLITS / SALAD OF DANDELION GREENS
ADAPTED FROM TOULOUSE-LAUTREC AND JOYANT'S
L'art de la cuisine, 1966.

In this recipe Toulouse-Lautrec calls for fresh dandelion greens gathered from a field in late January or February, just as the ground begins to thaw. It appears that the artist has taken poetic license, as there is usually not much in the way of greenery to be found so early in the year. This recipe should be prepared when the greens are fresh and locally available, which would generally be from early spring to early fall.

Serves 4

1	BUNCH DANDELION GREENS OR ARUGULA
½	TEASPOON SALT
3	TABLESPOONS OLIVE OR WALNUT OIL
1	TABLESPOON RED WINE VINEGAR
¼	TEASPOON COARSELY GROUND BLACK PEPPER
1	TEASPOON DIJON MUSTARD
2	HARD-BOILED EGGS, PEELED AND FINELY CHOPPED
1 ½	TABLESPOONS UNSALTED BUTTER
⅓	CUP DICED CANADIAN BACON

Wash the dandelion greens and dry them well. In a salad bowl, dissolve the salt in the oil and add the vinegar, pepper, and mustard. Mix well, add the chopped eggs, and mix again.

In a skillet, melt the butter and add the bacon. When it begins to brown slightly, remove from the heat. Just before serving, add the dandelion greens and bacon to the sauce and toss. Serve with toasted bread that has been rubbed with garlic.

SERPENT DU COUVENT /
THE CONVENT SERPENT

ADAPTED FROM TOULOUSE-LAUTREC AND JOYANT'S
L'art de la cuisine, 1966.

This wacky recipe is most revealing of Toulouse-Lautrec's whimsical and imaginative character. Forever seeking to surprise, delight, and *épater le bourgeois* (shock polite society), this dessert does a pretty good job of waking up the senses.

Scares 6–8

½	CUP UNSALTED BUTTER, SOFTENED
1 ¼	CUPS SUGAR
6	EGGS, BEATEN
	ZEST OF 1 LEMON OR ORANGE
1	TABLESPOON VANILLA EXTRACT
3	CUPS SIFTED ALL-PURPOSE FLOUR
2	RAISINS
¾	CUP ALMONDS, HALVED LENGTHWISE, OR AN EQUAL AMOUNT OF SLICED ALMONDS

In a mixing bowl, cream the butter and sugar until smooth and light. Gradually beat in the eggs, then the lemon or orange zest and vanilla. Add the flour 1 cup at a time and mix until it is fully incorporated. This should form a thick, firm dough. If the dough is too sticky, add more flour. Refrigerate, wrapped in wax paper, for 2–3 hours. (The dough must be chilled in order to be handled.)

Preheat the oven to 325°F.

Place the dough on a floured surface or on a sheet of wax paper and roll it into the shape of a serpent. Transfer to a greased and floured large baking sheet and arrange it in an S shape. Take the 2 raisins and make eyes. Cover the top with the almond halves, skin sides up, to resemble scales along the reptile's back. Bake 25–30 minutes, or until the serpent is fully cooked. Allow to cool before startling your guests.

[MENU NO. 14]

A Picnic at Fontainebleau

Omelette aux Champignons
MUSHROOM OMELETTE

Pâté en Croûte
PÂTÉ IN PASTRY

Poulet Rôti à l'Estragon
ROAST CHICKEN WITH TARRAGON

Côtelettes d'Agneau Panées et Grillées
BREADED GRILLED LAMB CHOPS

Asperges Sauce Vinaigrette
ASPARAGUS IN A VINAIGRETTE

Gâteau aux Framboises
RASPBERRY CAKE

Fruits de Saison
FRESH PEACHES AND GRAPES

Vins
WINES
Puligny-Montrachet / Château Beychevelle (Saint-Julien)

Café et Liqueurs
COFFEE AND LIQUEURS

THIS PICNIC DERIVES ITS INSPIRATION from one of the most famous *plein air* paintings in the history of art and features some of the food shown in the work—a golden-brown *Pâté en Croûte*, an inviting roast chicken, and a spread of freshly picked peaches and grapes. Set in the forest at Fontainebleau, a popular picnicking spot even today, this menu is informal, yet elegant, composed of easily transportable foods that utilize such inviting summer favorites as asparagus, raspberries, peaches, and grapes.

OMELETTE AUX CHAMPIGNONS / MUSHROOM OMELETTE
ADAPTED FROM THE
Nouveau manuel de la cuisine bourgeoise et économique, 1866.

In his *Grand dictionnaire de cuisine*, Dumas wrote: "There are people for whom an egg is an egg. This is a mistake. Two eggs that are laid at the same time, one by a hen that runs about in a garden, the other by a hen that eats straw in a farmyard, can be very different in taste and palatability."

Serves 2

- 1   CUP SLICED MUSHROOMS (CHANTERELLES, MORELS, CÈPES, OR CULTIVATED)
- 5   TABLESPOONS UNSALTED BUTTER
      SALT
      FRESHLY GROUND WHITE PEPPER
- 6   EGGS
- 1   TABLESPOON MILK OR WATER

In a skillet, sauté the mushrooms in 2 tablespoons of the butter until they are soft but still firm. Season with salt and pepper. In a mixing bowl, beat the eggs and add the milk or water. Melt the remaining 3 tablespoons of butter in an omelette pan. Swirl the pan so that the sides are coated with butter.

When the pan is hot, pour in the egg mixture and stir immediately, using a fork. The heat should be at medium-high.

Raise and lower the pan to control the heat. When the omelette has set a little, spoon the mushrooms across the middle. As the omelette continues to cook, run the fork around the edges to be sure the eggs are not sticking to the bottom or sides of the skillet. Roll up the omelette in the following manner: gripping the handle palm side up and raising it, fold the omelette over in thirds by bringing the outside edge to the inside, then slide the omelette onto a warm serving dish. Garnish with watercress.

PÂTÉ EN CROÛTE / PÂTÉ IN PASTRY
FROM AUDOT'S *La cuisinière de la campagne et de la ville*, 1851.

Pâté en croûte is a pâté covered with an unsweetened pastry. Depending on what the pâté filling is, different kinds of pastry are used. A *pâté de foie gras*, for instance, is often encased in a brioche dough, while a *pâté de canard* (duck) may be the filling for a lighter dough. *Pâtés en croûte* are molded in special tins with detachable sides, which makes removing the tin easy once the pâte is baked. It is rather time-consuming and somewhat tricky for the novice cook to attempt making the quintessentially French dish depicted in Monet's painting. For the adventurous cook with sufficient time and determination, here is a somewhat simplified version of *Pâté en Croûte*. (The other alternative is a nice, fresh 1-pound chunk of store-bought pâté; the kinds sold by specialty food stores are usually quite good.) *Bonne chance!*

Serves 10–12

PASTRY DOUGH
- 3   CUPS SIFTED ALL-PURPOSE FLOUR
- 2   EGGS
- ¾   CUP LARD (OR VEGETABLE SHORTENING)
- ½   TABLESPOONS SALT
        ICE WATER, IF NEEDED

Place the flour in a large bowl and make a well in the center. Place the eggs, salt, and lard into the well and gradually blend in the flour. Turn the dough out onto a board and knead it until it is smooth, adding 1–2 tablespoons of ice water if the dough is too dry. Form the dough into a ball and cover with plastic wrap. Chill for two hours or overnight.

Filling

3/4 POUND LEAN GROUND VEAL
3/4 POUND LEAN GROUND PORK
3   EGGS, BEATEN
2   TABLESPOONS FRESH FINES HERBES,
     MINCED (OR 1 TABLESPOON DRIED)
1/4 TEASPOON NUTMEG
1/4 TEASPOON CLOVES
1/4 TEASPOON GINGER
     SALT
     FRESHLY GROUND BLACK PEPPER

Combine the ground meats together in a bowl and add the salt and pepper, herbs, and spices. Add the beaten eggs and mix well. Correct seasoning if necessary.

Garniture

1/2 POUND CHICKEN LIVERS, CUT INTO
     1-INCH PIECES
4   THIN SLICES OF HAM
1   LARGE BONELESS CHICKEN BREAST,
     POUNDED FLAT AND CUT INTO THIN STRIPS
1 1/2 TEASPOONS FRESH THYME, CHOPPED FINE
1   TABLESPOON BRANDY OR PORT WINE

Egg Glaze

1   EGG, BEATEN
1   TEASPOON WATER (MORE IF NECESSARY)

Combine the beaten egg and water in a cup. Mix well. If the mixture is too thick, add more water.

To form the pâté:
Preheat the oven to 350°F.

On a floured surface, roll out 3/4 of the dough between two sheets of wax paper to a thickness of 1/4 inch. Reserve the remaining dough for the top of the pâté.

Line a 2-quart pâté mold or any metal 2-quart spring-form pan. Allow the pastry dough to hang over the rim of the mold about 1 inch.

Spread a little of the filling in the bottom of the lined pan, about 1/2-inch thick. Lay two slices of the ham on top of the filling. Cover the ham with the chicken liver pieces and top with the remaining slices of ham. Spread another layer of filling on top.

Place the strips of chicken over the ham and spread the remaining filling over the chicken until it is completely covered. Top with the thyme and sprinkle with brandy or port.

Roll out the rest of the dough. Before placing the dough on top of the pâté, paint the rim of the bottom pastry with the egg glaze so the two crusts will stick together. Trim the dough if necessary and pinch together the top and bottom crusts to seal. Paint the top crust with the egg glaze.

To release steam as the pâté bakes, pierce a 1/4-inch hole on top of the pâté. Place a piece of aluminum foil which has been formed into a cone shape into the hole. This funnel will help you determine when the pâté is done.

Bake the pâté on the middle rack of a preheated 350°F. oven for two hours. (It is a good idea to line the bottom of the oven with aluminum foil to catch any drips.) Pâté is done when the juices in the funnel hole have no trace of a rosy color. Remove the pâté from oven and let cool to room temperature. To remove from the mold, run a knife along the inside of the pan. The pastry may be stuck in several places. Release the spring-form pan and refrigerate the pâté for several hours before serving slightly chilled or at room temperature.

To serve, cut the pâté into slices about 1 1/2 to 2 inches thick. Serve with cornichons.

POULET RÔTI À L'ESTRAGON /
ROAST CHICKEN WITH TARRAGON
ADAPTED FROM AUDOT'S
La cuisinière de la campagne et de la ville, 1857.

Under the heading ESTRAGON in his dictionary of food, Dumas writes that this aromatic herb originally came from Siberia. And then, letting his preferences be known, the writer states that in his estimation, there is no good vinegar without tarragon; "and I invite the reader," announces Dumas, "to put it in his vinegar."

Serves 4–6

1	5 POUND ROASTING CHICKEN
½	LEMON
	SALT
	FRESHLY GROUND BLACK PEPPER
1	SMALL WHITE ONION, SLICED
2	TABLESPOONS UNSALTED BUTTER, SOFTENED
5	SPRIGS FRESH TARRAGON

Preheat the oven to 350°F.

After rinsing and drying the chicken, rub the cavity with the cut lemon. Sprinkle the cavity with salt and pepper and place the onion slices inside. Spread the softened butter on the outside of the chicken. Chop 2–3 sprigs of tarragon and sprinkle on top of the chicken. Season with salt and pepper and roast for about 1¼ hours. Baste with pan juices from time to time. The chicken is done when the drumstick juices run clear when pierced with a fork. Transfer to a serving dish and garnish with the remaining tarragon sprigs.

CÔTELETTES D'AGNEAU PANÉES ET GRILLÉES /
BREADED GRILLED LAMB CHOPS
ADAPTED FROM THE
Nouveau manuel de la cuisine bourgeoise et économique, 1866.

Serves 4

4	LARGE LAMB CHOPS
2	TABLESPOONS VEGETABLE OIL
	SALT
	FRESHLY GROUND WHITE PEPPER
½	CUP DRIED UNSEASONED BREAD CRUMBS
	MAÎTRE D'HÔTEL SAUCE (RECIPE FOLLOWS)
4	SPRIGS FRESH ROSEMARY (GARNISH)

Preheat the broiler.

Brush the chops with the oil, then season with salt and pepper and coat in the bread crumbs. Broil the chops on both sides according to the desired degree of doneness. Remove the chops to a warm serving dish and serve the *maître d'hôtel* sauce in a dollop on the side or on top of each chop.

MAÎTRE D'HÔTEL SAUCE
Makes 3/4 cup

2	TABLESPOONS MINCED FRESH FINES HERBES (SEE NOTE ON PAGE 40)
½	CUP UNSALTED BUTTER, SOFTENED
2	TEASPOONS LEMON JUICE
2	PINCHES OF SALT

With a mortar and pestle, crush the herbs and beat in the butter and lemon juice. Season with salt and blend until smooth.

ASPERGES SAUCE VINAIGRETTE / ASPARAGUS IN A VINAIGRETTE

ADAPTED FROM DUBOIS'S *La cuisine classique*, 1867

The entry for asparagus in the *Grand dictionnaire de cuisine* is classic Dumas. He begins the section by stating that there is no point in describing this plant because it is known by everyone. He adds that carnivorous animals, such as cats and dogs, like this vegetable very much. Dumas also includes an Italian expression relating to asparagus. He writes that when someone wanted something to be done in a hurry one would say, "Do that in less time than it would take to cook asparagus."

Serves 2–4

1 POUND FRESH THIN ASPARAGUS
½ CUP SHALLOT VINAIGRETTE (SEE PAGE 78)

Trim off the rough bottom stems of the asparagus. Bring a large pot of salted water to a boil, add the asparagus, and cook, uncovered, for about 8 minutes. Test a spear for doneness. It should be tender yet firm. Pour off the boiling water and remove the asparagus from the pot with tongs, being careful not to crush the tips. Allow to cool in a colander and arrange on a serving platter. Pour the vinaigrette on top and serve warm or chilled.

GÂTEAU AUX FRAMBOISES / RASPBERRY CAKE

ADAPTED FROM AUDOT'S
La cuisinière de la campagne et de la ville, 1857.

Serves 6

¾ CUP GRANULATED SUGAR
3 EGGS, BEATEN
2 CUPS SIFTED ALL-PURPOSE FLOUR
2 TEASPOONS BAKING POWDER
DASH OF SALT
½ CUP MILK
1 ½ TABLESPOONS GRAND MARNIER OR KIRSCH
1 PINT FRESH RASPBERRIES
2 TEASPOONS SUPERFINE SUGAR

Preheat the oven to 350°F.

In a large mixing bowl, beat the granulated sugar and eggs. Stir the flour, baking powder, and salt together and slowly add to the sugar-egg mixture, alternating with the milk. Mix well and add the liqueur, continuing to mix. Pick over the berries to remove stems or leaves, but do not wash them. Sprinkle with the superfine sugar and add to the cake batter, folding carefully so that the berries are not broken. Pour the batter into a greased and floured 8-inch cake pan and bake for 25–30 minutes. Cool and unmold the cake. Serve as is, with vanilla ice cream, or with a berry sorbet.

| Menu Nº. 15 |

A Rowers' Luncheon

Bisque d'Ecrevisses
CRAYFISH BISQUE

Pommes de Terre Sautées aux Fines Herbes
SAUTÉED POTATOES WITH HERBS

Petits Pois au Lard
GREEN PEAS WITH BACON

Rougets Grillés
GRILLED RED MULLET

Coq au Vin
CHICKEN IN RED WINE

Fromages Assortis
ASSORTED CHEESES: CAMEMBERT, GRUYÈRE, ROBLOCHON

Tarte Tatin
UPSIDE-DOWN APPLE TART

Vins
WINES
Montagny (Chalonnais) / Ladoix (Côte de Beaune)

Café et Liqueurs
COFFEE AND LIQUEURS

A COMPANION PIECE of sorts to the *Luncheon of the Boating Party* menu (page 35), this one presents the typical dishes found on the menus of many hotels and restaurants that dotted the banks of the Seine in the last century and catered to devotees of "le rowing." The growing vogue for water sports on the Seine drew Parisians to the outskirts of Paris, where they dined simply and heartily on such dishes as *Pommes de Terre Sautées aux Fines Herbes*, *Petits Pois au Lard*, *Rougets Grilles*, and *Tarte Tatin*, the nineteenth-century apple pie *par excellence*.

BISQUE D'ECREVISSES / CRAYFISH BISQUE
Adapted from Audot's
La cuisinière de la campagne et de la ville, 1857.

Crayfish Bisque was among the most popular bisques at the time of the Impressionists; it appears in the recipe indexes of most cookbooks printed in the mid- to late nineteenth century. During the eighteenth and nineteenth centuries, seafood bisques made of oyster, shrimp, and lobster were generally thickened with rice. As the use of cream as a thickening agent increased later in the nineteenth century, rice was dropped from the dish.

Serves 4–6

1	TABLESPOON UNSALTED BUTTER
1	TABLESPOON VEGETABLE OIL
1	SMALL ONION
1	CARROT
1 ½	POUNDS CRAYFISH (CLEANED JUMBO SHRIMP CAN BE SUBSTITUTED)
¼	CUP COGNAC
½	CUP DRY WHITE WINE
1	BOUQUET GARNI (SEE PAGE 110; USE PARSLEY, THYME, AND BAY LEAVES)
4	CUPS FISH OR CHICKEN STOCK
½	CUP HEAVY CREAM OR HALF-AND-HALF
3	EGG YOLKS, BEATEN
	SALT
	FRESHLY GROUND WHITE PEPPER

In a large saucepan, heat the butter and oil and sauté the onion and carrots. Do not brown. Add the crayfish and cook, stirring continuously, for 5 minutes. Add the cognac and ignite. Add the wine and *bouquet garni* and simmer, covered, for about 10 minutes. Remove from the heat. Discard the *bouquet garni.*

Transfer the crayfish to a bowl. When they are cool enough to handle, remove the meat from the tails and purée along with the diced sautéed vegetables. Put the mixture back into the saucepan and add the stock. Bring to a boil and remove from heat.

In a bowl, mix the cream and egg yolks. Add a little of the stock to the egg and cream mixture and blend well with a wire whisk. Pour it into the saucepan containing the rest of the soup. Return to low heat, stirring until the soup thickens a little. Strain through a fine sieve. Season with salt and pepper, reheat, and serve immediately.

POMMES DE TERRE SAUTÉES AUX FINES HERBES / SAUTÉED POTATOES WITH HERBS
Adapted from Dubois's *La cuisine classique*, 1867.

Serves 4

4	LARGE BOILING POTATOES, PEELED
3	TABLESPOONS UNSALTED BUTTER
	SALT
	FRESHLY GROUND BLACK PEPPER
1	TABLESPOON MINCED FRESH **FINES HERBES** (SEE NOTE ON PAGE 40)

Cook the potatoes in boiling salted water for 15 minutes. Slice and allow to cool. In a a sauté pan, melt the butter and add the potatoes. Season with salt and pepper and cook, turning frequently, until the potatoes are golden brown. Sprinkle with the *fines herbes* and place on a serving dish. Pour the melted butter over the potatoes and serve.

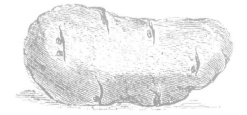

PETITS POIS AU LARD /
GREEN PEAS WITH BACON

ADAPTED FROM DUBOIS'S *La cuisine classique*, 1867.

Under the heading COCHON (literally pig, not pork) in his *Grand dictionnaire de cuisine*, Dumas quotes Grimod de la Reynière, who said of the pig, "It is the king of the unclean animals. It is the one whose empire is the most universal, and whose qualities are least in dispute. Without it there would be no bacon, and consequently no cookery; without it no ham, no sausage, no andouille, no black pudding, and therefore no charcutiers."

Serves 6–8

2	POUNDS FRESH SHELLED PEAS, COOKED UNTIL TENDER
3	TABLESPOONS UNSALTED BUTTER
1	SMALL ONION, MINCED
⅓	CUP BLANCHED BACON, DICED
½	TEASPOON SUGAR
	SALT

If fresh peas are not available, substitute two 10-ounce packages of frozen peas that have been thawed in the following manner: put the peas in a colander and run hot water over them for about 30 seconds. This will "reconstitute" them as cooked fresh peas.

In a sauté pan, melt the butter and add the onion and bacon. Cook, stirring continuously, until the onion is soft. Add the peas, sugar, and salt. Mix well and simmer over gentle heat for about 5 minutes. If needed, add 1–2 tablespoons of water. Transfer the peas to a serving dish and serve hot.

ROUGETS GRILLÉS / GRILLED RED MULLET

ADAPTED FROM AUDOT'S
La cuisinière de la campagne et de la ville, 1857.

Serves 4

4	SMALL RED MULLETS, ABOUT 1 POUND EACH, SCALED AND GUTTED
1	CAN BEER
½	CUP ALL-PURPOSE FLOUR
½	CUP OLIVE OIL
2	TEASPOONS DRIED ROSEMARY LEAVES
	SALT
½	LEMON
1	WHOLE LEMON, CUT INTO WEDGES (GARNISH)
	FRESH ROSEMARY SPRIGS (GARNISH)

Preheat the broiler.

Lay the fish in a shallow dish or pie plate filled with beer. Let them sit for a few minutes, then drain. Coat the fish in the flour, brush with the olive oil, and sprinkle with the rosemary leaves. Broil the fish under medium heat for about 5 minutes on each side, brushing them lightly with the olive oil several times during the cooking. Season with salt and transfer to a serving dish. Squeeze the juice of ½ lemon over the fish and serve garnished with lemon wedges and rosemary sprigs.

COQ AU VIN / CHICKEN IN RED WINE
ADAPTED FROM DUBOIS'S *La cuisine classique*, 1867.

Poultry (*volaille*), which includes turkey, duck, goose, and capon, was an important part of the Parisian diet during the last century. In the menus outlined in *Les 366 menus de Baron Brisse*, chicken appears nearly seventy times.

Serves 4–6

- 2 TABLESPOONS VEGETABLE OIL
- 3 TABLESPOONS UNSALTED BUTTER
- 20 PEARL ONIONS
- ¼ POUND BACON, CUT INTO STRIPS
- 1 LARGE FRYING CHICKEN, CUT INTO 8 PIECES
  SALT AND PEPPER
- ¼ CUP BRANDY
- 1 BOTTLE (750 ML) DRY RED WINE
- 2 TABLESPOONS ALL-PURPOSE FLOUR
- 2 CLOVES GARLIC, MINCED
- 1 BOUQUET GARNI (SEE PAGE 110)

In a sauté pan, heat half of the oil and butter and cook the onions until they are golden. Add the bacon and cook until it is transparent. Remove the onions and bacon from the pan and set aside. Put the chicken pieces in the sauté pan and brown on all sides. Season with salt and pepper. Sprinkle with the brandy and ignite.

In a saucepan, heat the wine. Sprinkle the flour over the chicken and add the hot wine to the casserole. Add the garlic and *bouquet garni* and simmer over low heat for about 45 minutes. When the chicken is fully cooked, discard the *bouquet garni* and add the bacon and onions. Transfer everything to a deep serving dish and serve at once.

TARTE TATIN / UPSIDE-DOWN APPLE TART
ADAPTED FROM JOYES'S *Les carnets de cuisine de Monet*, 1989.

Serves 6–8

- ½ RECIPE **PÂTE BRISÉE SUCRÉE**
  (SEE PAGE 41)
- ½ CUP LIGHT BROWN SUGAR
- 2 POUNDS TART APPLES, PEELED, CORED,
  AND CUT INTO THICK SLICES
- ½ CUP UNSALTED BUTTER, SOFTENED
  GROUND CINNAMON AND NUTMEG
  (OPTIONAL)

Preheat oven to 400°F.

Roll out the pastry into a 9-inch round. Butter the bottom of a 9-inch pie pan and sprinkle with half of the sugar. Arrange the apple slices in the pan, top with the remaining sugar, and dot with butter. Sprinkle with cinnamon and nutmeg if desired.

Cover the apples with the pastry, being sure to tuck the dough into the sides of the pan. Bake for 30 minutes. Invert the pie onto a serving plate and cool before serving. Serve with vanilla ice cream or *crème Chantilly* (see page 65).

BIBLIOGRAPHY

Almanach des ménagères et gastronomes. Paris, c. 1878.

Aron, Jean-Paul. *Le mangeur de XIXième siècle.* Paris: Editions Payot, 1989.

Audot, Louis Eustache. *French Domestic Cookery, Combining Elegance with Economy.* New York: Harper Brothers, 1855.

———. *La cuisinière de la campagne et de la ville.* Paris: Bernardin-Béchet et Fils Editeurs, 8th edition, 1888.

Baudelaire, Charles. *The Painter of Modern Life and Other Essays.* London: Phaidon Press, 1964.

Bernard, Françoise. *Le livre d'or: La cuisine de tous les Français.* Paris: Hachette, 1985.

Blunden, Maria and Godfrey. *Impressionists and Impressionism.* New York: Skira/Rizzoli, 1970.

Brillat-Savarin, Jean-Anthelme. *Physiologie du Goût: Méditations de gastronomie transcendante.* 2 vols. Paris: A. Sautelet et Cie, 1826.

Brisse, Baron (Léon). *Les 366 menus de Baron Brisse avec 120 recettes et un calendrier nutritif.* Paris: E. Dentu Libraire Editeur, 1875.

Brookner, Anita. *The Genius of the Future: Studies in French Art Criticism.* London, New York: Phaidon, 1971.

Carême, Mélanie. *Le parfait Cordon Bleu: Cuisine bourgeoise et petite cuisine des ménages.* Paris: Arthème Fayard Editeur, c. 1880.

Carley, Eliane Ame. *Classics from a French Kitchen.* New York: Crown, 1983.

Cauderlier. *L'économie culinaire.* Brussels: Alexandre Moens, 1889.

Child, Julia, Louisette Bertholle, and Simone Beck. *Mastering the Art of French Cooking,* Vol. 1. New York: Alfred A. Knopf, 1961.

Child, Julia and Simone Beck. *Mastering the Art of French Cooking,* Vol. 2. New York: Alfred A. Knopf, 1970.

Clark, T. J. *The Painting of Modern Life: The Art of Manet and His Followers.* Princeton: Princeton University Press, 1984.

Clayson, Hollis. *Painted Love.* New Haven and London: Yale University Press, 1991.

Conrad, Barnaby. *Absinthe: History in a Bottle.* San Francisco: Chronicle Books, 1988.

Courtine, Robert, and Jean Desmur. *Anthologie de la littérature gastronomique: Les écrivains à table.* Paris: Editions de Trevise, 1970.

Courtine, Robert. *Grand livre de la France à table.* Paris: Pierre Bordas et Fils, Editeurs, 1972.

Crespelle, Jean-Paul. *Guide de la France impressioniste.* Paris: Editions Hazan, 1990.

———. *La vie quotidienne des impressionistes 1863–1883.* Paris: Hachette, 1981.

Davidson, Alan and Jane. *Dumas on Food: Recipes and Anecdotes from the Classic Grand Dictionnaire de Cuisine.* Oxford: Oxford University Press, 1987.

Dubois, Urbain. *La cuisine d'aujourd'hui.* 12th edition. Paris: E. Flammarion, 1886.

———. *La cuisine classique.* Paris: E. Dentu Libraire Editeur, 1886.

———. *Nouvelle cuisine bourgeoise pour la ville et pour la campagne.* 8th edition. Paris: Bernardin-Béchet et Fils, 1888.

Dumas, Alexandre. *Grand dictionnaire de cuisine.* Paris: Alphonse Lemerre, 1873.

Durandeau, Mme. C. *Guide de la bonne cuisine.* Paris: Vermot, Editeur, 1887.

Emmeline, Raymond. *Le nouveau livre de cuisine, recettes pratiques.* Paris: Fermin-Didot et Cie, 1888.

Fitzgibbon, Theodora. *A Taste of Paris.* Boston: Houghton Mifflin, 1974.

Friedrich, Otto. *Olympia: Paris in the Age of Manet.* New York: Harper Collins, 1992.

Gouffé, Jules. *Le livre de cuisine: La cuisine de ménage et la grande cuisine*. Paris: Hachette, 1867.

Hanson, Lawrence. *Renoir: The Man, the Painter and His World*. London: Leslie Frewin, Ltd., 1970.

Herbert, Robert L. *Impressionism: Art, Leisure and Parisian Society*. New Haven and London: Yale University Press, 1988.

L'Impressionisme. Paris: Fernand Hazan, Dictionnaire de Poche, 1972.

Joanne, Adolphe. *Le guide Parisien*. Paris: Hachette, 1863.

Joyes, Claire. *Les carnets de cuisine de Claude Monet*. Paris: Editions de Chêne, 1989.

Leveques, Jean-Jacques. *Les années impressionistes*. Paris: ACR Editions Internationale, 1990.

Maupassant, Guy de. *La maison Tellier: Une partie de campagne et autres contes*. Paris: Garnier-Flammarion, 1980.

———. *The Short Stories of Guy de Maupassant*. Translated by Michael Monahan. New York: Modern Library, 1925.

Nouvel manuel de la cuisine bourgeoise et economique. Paris, 1866.

Oliver, Raymond. *La cuisine*. Paris: Editions Bordas, 1967

Stern, Barbara, ed. *The Pleasures of Paris: From Daumier to Picasso*. Boston: Museum of Fine Arts, Boston and David R. Godine, 1991.

Rewald, John. *The History of Impressionism*. New York: The Museum of Modern Art, 1973.

Scotto Sisters and Annie Hubert Bare. *The Heritage French Cookbook*. New York: Random House, 1991.

Stuckey, Charles F. *Monet: A Retrospective*. New York: Park Lane, 1985.

Henri de Toulouse-Lautrec and Maurice Joyant. *The Art of Cuisine*. New York: Henry Holt; Lausanne: Edita-Lazarus, 1966.

Vicaire, Georges. *Bibliographie gastronomique*. London: Holland Press, 1890.

Weckler, Charles. *Impressions of Giverny: Monet's World*. New York: Harry N. Abrams, 1990.

Zola, Emile. *The Masterpiece*. New York: Howell Soskin, 1946.

———. *Le ventre de Paris*. Paris: Folio, 1964.

LIST OF ILLUSTRATIONS

GENERAL INDEX

RECIPE INDEX